HISTORY

-OF-

LEITERSBURG DISTRICT
WASHINGTON COUNTY, MARYLAND

INCLUDING

ITS ORIGINAL LAND TENURE; FIRST SETTLEMENT;
MATERIAL DEVELOPMENT; RELIGIOUS,
EDUCATIONAL, POLITICAL, AND GENERAL HISTORY;
AND BIOGRAPHICAL SKETCHES

HERBERT C. BELL

HERITAGE BOOKS
2007

HERITAGE BOOKS
AN IMPRINT OF HERITAGE BOOKS, INC.

Books, CDs, and more—Worldwide

For our listing of thousands of titles see our website
at
www.HeritageBooks.com

Published 2007 by
HERITAGE BOOKS, INC.
Publishing Division
65 East Main Street
Westminster, Maryland 21157-5026

Copyright © 1898 Herbert C. Bell

All rights reserved. No part of this book may be reproduced or transmitted in any form or by any means, electronic or mechanical, including photocopying, recording or by any information storage and retrieval system without written permission from the author, except for the inclusion of brief quotations in a review.

International Standard Book Number: 978-0-7884-3481-5

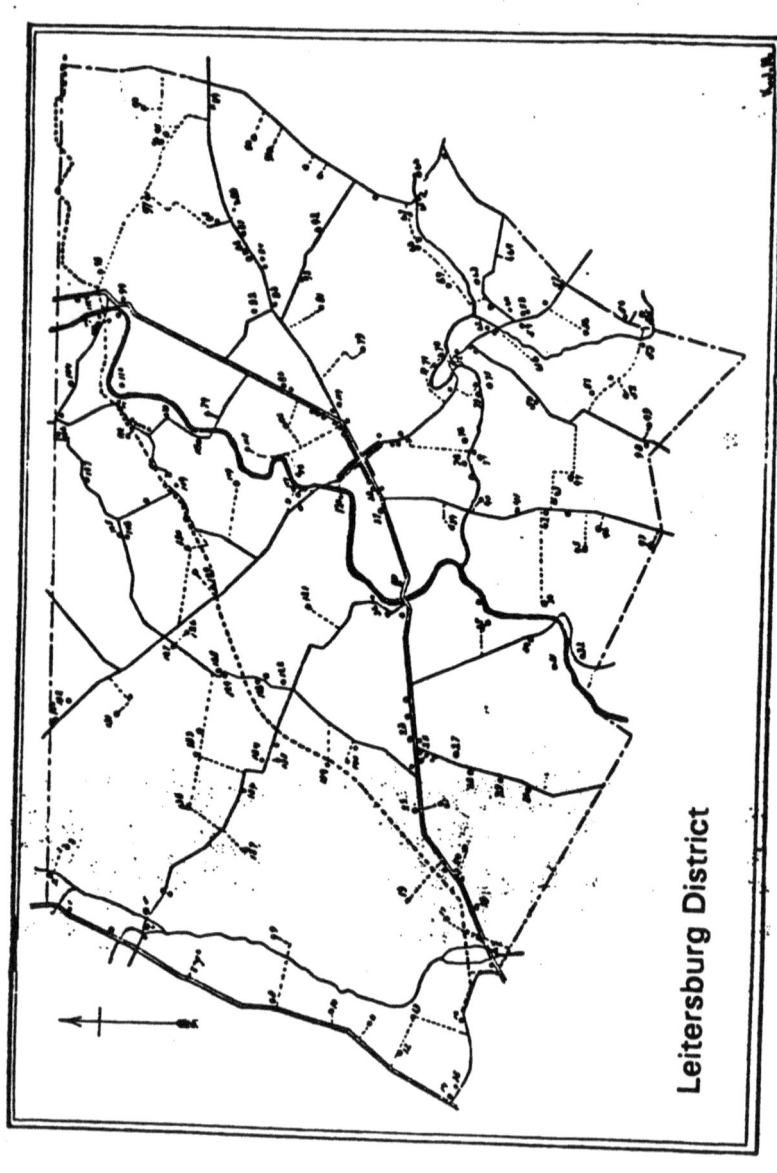

EXPLANATIONS.

APPROXIMATE scale, one inch to a mile. Continuous lines indicate public roads; double lines, turnpikes; broken lines, private roads; the heavy broken line, the old Nicholson's Gap road.

REAL ESTATE OWNERS.

1. John Wingert.
2. Isaac Hykes.
3. J. H. Hykes.
4, 5. Henry F. Lehman.
6. Isaac Shank.
7. Cressler Brothers.
8, 9. William S. Young.
10. Mrs. William S. Young.
11. Abraham Lehman.
12. William G. Young.
13. Daniel N. Scheller.
14. Paradise School.
15. M. L. Trovinger.
16. Longmeadows Church.
17. Samuel Hykes.
18. O. H. Ragan.
19. Jacob B. Lehman.
20. William H. Hykes.
21. Henry M. Jacobs.
22. Heirs of Frederick Ziegler.
23. John C. Miller.
24. David Ziegler (Startown Postoffice).
25. Edward M. White.
26. Mt. Union School.
27. Lewis H. Myers.
28. William G. Martin.
29. Samuel Boward.
30. John D. Spessard.
31. Simon Clopper.
32. Henry F. Unger.
33, 42. Samuel Hartle.
34. Henry and Frederick Hartle.
35. Alveh L. Stockslager.
36. Frank D. Bell.
37. George H. Wolfinger.
38. Joseph Barkdoll.
39. Harvey J. Hartle.
40, 41. Levi Hartle.
43. Clinton W. Hartle.
44. B. F. Spessard.
45. J. H. Wishard.
46. J. C. Stouffer.
47. George T. McKee.
48. Martin C. Funk.
49. Daniel Beck.
50. Lewis Miller.
51. Levi L. Ridenour.
52. Mrs. Magdalene Neff.
53. Curtis Fogler.
54. John B. Newcomer.
55. Samuel Newcomer.
56. John Wishard.
57. George A. Beard.
58. George W. Coss.
59. Martin's School.
60. Jacob Needy.
61. Joseph Martin.
62. Julia and Lydia Bell.
63, 64. Daniel W. Durboraw.
65. Rudolph Charles.
66. C. L. G. Anderson.
67. Charles B. and Levi B. Wolfinger.
68. Jacob B. Stoner.
69. Mrs. Elizabeth Stoner.
70, 92. Immanuel and Katie E. Martin.
71. Henry Martin.
72. George H. Bowman (Mills Postoffice).
73. (S. E. of Leitersburg) Freeland W. Anderson.
73. (North of Leitersburg) Samuel Martin.
74. Daniel Oller.
75. Heirs of Henry G. Clopper.
76. Joseph and John B. Barkdoll.
77. Claggett Hartle.
78. Daniel Hoover.
79. Upton Clopper.
80. Solomon Stephey.
81. Mrs. Margaret Leather.
82. Daniel V. Shank.
83. Joseph Wishard.
84. Leonard Senger.
85. Kemp M. Bell.
86. Pleasant Hill School.
87. Albert Stoner.
88. Heirs of Daniel Harshman.
89. Mrs. Mary M. Newcomer.
90. William F. Ridenour.

EXPLANATIONS.

91. William H. Stevenson.
93. Daniel R. Grove.
94. William H. Hoffman.
95. Mrs. Naucy Hoffman.
96. E. Keller Mentzer.
97. Joseph M. Bell.
98. Daniel S. Wolfinger.
99. Heirs of John Eshleman.
100. John H. Miller.
101. Otho Kahl.
102. William H. Barkdoll.
103. Benjamin Shockey (Rock Forge).
104. Augustus Shiffler.
105. Franklin M. Strite.
106. Jacobs Church.
107. Daniel Hoover.
108. Mrs. Martha H. Leiter.
109. New Harmony School.
110. Lewis Lecron.
111. John Kriner.
112. Mrs. Fanny Strite.
113. Isaac Needy.
114. Heirs of Joseph Strite.
115. Hiram D. Middlekauff.
116. John A. Bell.
117. Samuel Strite.
118. John Summer.
119. (West of Leitersburg) George F. Ziegler.
119. (N. E. of Leitersburg) C. C. Hollinger.
120. Heirs of David Strite.
121. Henry L. Strite.
122. Mrs. Mary A. Gilbert.
123. William H. Kreps.
124. Noah E. Shank.
125. Miller's Church.
126. Daniel W. Martin.
127. John O. Wolfinger.
129. Heirs of Joseph Strite.
130. John S. Strite.
131. John F. Strite.
132. Samuel McH. Cook.
133. W. Harvey Hykes.
134. Casper Linderman.
135. Mrs. Laura K. Ziegler.
136. Rock Hill School.
137. David H. Wolfinger.
138. Mrs. Mary A. Jacobs.
139. Mrs. Mary A. Hykes.
140. Henry M. Jacobs.

CONTENTS.

INTRODUCTION.

WASHINGTON COUNTY, MARYLAND.

Situation and Extent—General History—Political Organization—Internal Improvements—Town and Village Growth 9-18

CHAPTER I.

EARLY LAND TENURE AND SETTLEMENT.

Antietam—Prehistoric Remains—Longmeadows—Skipton-on-Craven—Deceit—Darling's Sale—Lambert's Park—Downing's Lot—Chester—Well Taught—Allamangle—All That's Left—Rich Barrens—Perry's Retirement—Huckleberry Hall—Dry Spring—Burkhart's Lot—Scant Timber—Father's Good Will—Elysian Fields—The Farmer's Blessing—Addition to Cumberland—Turkey Buzzard—Cumberland—Smaller Tracts—Adjustment of Boundaries—Mason and Dixon's Line. 19-50

CHAPTER II.

SOCIAL AND MATERIAL DEVELOPMENT.

Language, Dress, Etc.—Slavery—Erection and Boundaries of Leitersburg District—Politics—"In War Times"—Agricultural Development—Postal Facilities—Public Roads—Bridges—Turnpikes—Mills—Rock Forge—Distilleries—Tanneries, Textile Manufactures, Etc. 51-101

CHAPTER III.

LEITERSBURG.

Early History—The Town Plot—The Village in 1830—Business Interests — Secret Societies — Municipal Incorporation — Population. 102-112

CHAPTER IV.

CHURCHES.

Antietam Lutheran Church—Jacobs Lutheran Church—St. Paul's Lutheran Church, Leitersburg—St. James Reformed Church, Leitersburg—Miller's Mennonite Church—Longmeadows German Baptist Church—Reformed Mennonite—River Brethren—United Brethren Church, Leitersburg—Methodist Episcopal Church, Leitersburg 113-142

CONTENTS.

CHAPTER V.
SCHOOLS.

"The Hollow House"—Martin's School—Leitersburg Schools—The Jacobs Church School—"Jacob Miller's School House"—Paradise—Rock Hill—Pleasant Hill—New Harmony—Mt. Union—General Statistics 143-154

CHAPTER VI.
BIOGRAPHICAL SKETCHES.

. . . . 155-331

INDEX 333-337

INTRODUCTION.

WASHINGTON COUNTY, MARYLAND.

SITUATION AND EXTENT—GENERAL HISTORY—POLITICAL ORGANIZATION—INTERNAL IMPROVEMENTS—TOWN AND VILLAGE GROWTH.

A NOTICEABLE feature of the Appalachian mountain system is the great valley that extends from Vermont to Alabama, bounded on either side by parallel ranges and crossed by the largest rivers of the Atlantic slope in the United States—the Hudson, the Delaware, the Susquehanna, the Potomac, and the James. The section between the Susquehanna and the Potomac is called the Cumberland valley, in which the larger part of Washington County is situated. It is bounded on the south by the Potomac river; on the east the South mountain separates it from the adjacent county of Frederick; Mason and Dixon's Line is the northern limit of its territory, which terminates at Sideling Hill creek on the west. The county has a maximum length of forty-four miles; in breadth it varies from a mile and a half at Hancock to twenty-eight miles at the base of the South mountain.

The basin of the Potomac river embraces the whole of Washington County, from which its principal affluents are the Conococheague and Antietam. Both rise in Pennsylvania. The former pursues an extremely winding course through the geological formation known as slate or shale and joins the Potomac at Williamsport; the latter traverses a limestone region and terminates its course near Sharpsburg.

GENERAL HISTORY.

The Indian occupation of Western Maryland is perpetuated in the names of its streams—Potomac, Conococheague, Antietam, Tonoloway, Monocacy, etc. Indian village sites, burial grounds, and battle-fields have been identified in various parts of Washington County. About the year 1736 a sanguinary battle occurred at the mouth of the Conococheague between the Delawares and Catawbas, in which the former were disastrously defeated. Schlatter, writing of the Conococheague region in 1749, says: "In this neighborhood there are still many Indians, who are well disposed and very obliging and are not disinclined toward the Christians when they are not made drunk by strong drink."

The upper Potomac was explored at an early period in the history of Maryland, but nearly a century elapsed after the founding of St. Mary's before the present territory of Washington County was formally opened to settlement. The sale of lands west of the South mountain was first authorized in 1733. The Proprietary reserved the Manor of Conococheague, a tract of eleven thousand acres. The largest individual estate in the county was Ringgold's Manor (twenty thousand acres); Chew's farm, Longmeadows, Montpelier, the Chapline, Jacques, and Hughes lands were also extensive tracts.

Two converging streams of immigration contributed to the early settlement of Washington County. There was a movement of population, principally English in nationality, across the South mountain from the older settlements of Maryland, while the German communities of southeastern Pennsylvania also contributed a large contingent, which found its way thither through Lancaster, York, and the Cumberland valley. To the relative numerical strength of the different nationalities composing the early population there is perhaps no better index than religious preferences. The Church of England was an established provincial institution and one of the first places of public worship in the county was an Episcopal chapel, situated near Chapel Woods school in Funkstown District; but the adherents of this faith, while generally wealthy and influential, were not numerous, and no other English church existed in the county before the Revolution. There was a German Reformed congregation at Conococheague as early as 1747, at Hagerstown in 1766, and at Salem in 1768; a German Lutheran congregation at Antietam in 1754, at Sharpsburg in 1768, at Hagerstown in 1769, and at Funkstown in 1771. German Mennonites and Baptists were also represented before the Revolution.

Washington County was the scene of important military operations during the French and Indian war. Braddock's army, which rendezvoused at Frederick, crossed the county on its march to Fort Cumberland in the campaign which terminated in disastrous defeat on the Monongahela, July 9, 1755. A general panic ensued; in the Conococheague settlement numbers of people deserted their homes and retired for safety to the interior of the Province. As Fort Cumberland was too far to the westward to afford adequate protection Governor Sharpe built Fort Frederick, an extensive fortification with massive stone walls near the Potomac fourteen miles above the Conococheague. Here a garrison was stationed until the close of hostilities. Parties of Indians still devastated the frontier, however, especially in 1763, when a second exódus similar to that of 1755 occurred. But in 1764 the allied tribes of Pontiac's confederacy were finally defeated and the western frontier of Maryland at length enjoyed the benefits of undisturbed tranquility.

After the close of the French and Indian War the development of Washington County was rapid. The population increased, and the cultivated area was greatly extended. The number of mills multiplied and flour became a staple commodity for export. Towns were founded and soon became local centers of business and industry. The mineral resources of the county were also developed: the Jacques Furnace in Indian Spring District, Mt. Aetna at the South mountain, and the Antietam Iron Works were all in operation at this period. A number of important public roads were opened to facilitate internal communication and the transportation of the varied products of the farm, the mill, and the forge to distant markets.

In the war for American independence the people of Washington County bore an honorable part. The Stamp Act of 1765 was practically nullified in Frederick County by the action of the county court and the revenue measures by which it was followed were successfully frustrated. "On Saturday, the 2d of July, 1774," as reported in the Maryland *Gazette*, "about eight hundred of the principal inhabitants of the upper part of Frederick County assembled at Elizabeth-Town and being deeply impressed with a sense of the danger to which their natural and constitutional rights and privileges were exposed by the arbitrary measures of the British Parliament," expressed their sentiments in a series of resolutions in which the Boston Port Bill was denounced, the suspension of all commercial relations with Great Britain and the holding of a Continental Congress were advised, etc. On the 12th of September, 1775, a Committee of Observation was elected, which exercised general executive and judicial functions within its jurisdiction until the 3d of March, 1777. It supervised elections, regulated the militia, tried offenders and suspected persons, etc. Of the representation of the county in the field it is possible to speak only in general terms. In addition to a full complement of regular troops the militia was also called out and rendered efficient service. Cannon were manufactured in the county for the State troops and military supplies of various kinds were also obtained here. Fort Frederick was used for a time as a place of detention for prisoners of war.

In the War of 1812 the county was represented at the battles of Bladensburg and Baltimore and in the Canada campaign. After the battle of Bladensburg General Ringgold mustered his brigade at Boonsboro but its services were not considered necessary by the Secretary of War.

The Civil War was an eventful period in the history of Washington County. It was at a farm house near the Potomac opposite Harper's Ferry that John Brown collected the band of twenty-one men with which he seized the United States arsenal at that place. In June, 1861, ten thousand Federal troops marched through the county and occupied Harper's Ferry. In the Maryland campaign of 1862 the Confederate army occupied Frederick on the 6th of September; here several divisions were detached for the reduction of Harper's Ferry, while the main body crossed the South mountain. The Federal army reached Frederick on the 12th and continued in pursuit; its advance was disputed by the enemy at the passes of the South mountain, where a battle was fought on the 14th of September. The Confederates then concentrated their forces west of the Antietam in the vicinity of Sharpsburg, and here on the 17th of September occurred the greatest battle ever fought on Maryland soil. Eighty thousand Federal troops and forty thousand Confederates were engaged, and the aggregate loss in killed and wounded was twenty thousand. In the Confederate invasion of 1863 Lee's army of eighty-five thousand men marched through Washington County, which was also the scene of its retreat after the battle of Gettysburg. Of minor military movements the most important were Stuart's

INTRODUCTION. 13

raid of October, 1862, and McCausland's raid of July, 1864, when Chambersburg was burned. The county had a large representation in the Federal army and the sentiment of its people was overwhelmingly favorable to the Union.

POLITICAL ORGANIZATION.

From 1658 to 1776 Western Maryland was successively included in the geographical limits of Charles, Prince George's, and Frederick Counties, erected in 1658, 1695, and 1748, respectively. On the 26th of July, 1776, the Provincial Convention of Maryland divided Frederick County into three election districts, designated as the Upper, Middle, and Lower. The first and most extensive included the present territory of Washington, Allegany, and Garrett Counties; the second, Frederick and part of Carroll; the third, Montgomery. Each of these divisions was constituted a separate county by an ordinance passed on the 6th of September, 1776. Washington County thus included all that part of the State west of the South mountain until 1789, when Allegany County was erected.

The first court house of Washington County stood in the center of the public square in Hagerstown. It was a two-story structure; the court-room and public offices were on the second floor, while the first was used as a market house. In 1816 the Legislature authorized the selection of a new site and the erection of a new building, which was accordingly located at the corner of Washington and Jonathan streets. On the night of December 6, 1871, it was destroyed by fire. The present court house, a substantial and imposing brick edifice, was erected in 1872-74.

The first county prison was a log building. The second was situated on East Franklin street, nearly opposite the market house. The present jail is located on North Jonathan street and was built in 1857-58.

The county almshouse was located for many years in Hagerstown, at the corner of Locust and Bethel streets. In 1878 John Nicodemus presented to the county a farm near Hagerstown upon which commodious buildings for the accommodation of the indigent and insane have been erected by the county commissioners.

At March term, 1749, the Frederick County court established five hundreds in the territory subsequently embraced in Washington County. Antietam extended from the Potomac to the Temporary Line between South mountain and Antietam creek. Marsh and Salisbury included the territory between Antietam and Conococheague; Marsh extended from the Potomac to "the road that leads from Wolgamot's mill to Stull's," and Salisbury from that road to the Temporary Line. Conococheague extended from the Conococheague to Big Tonoloway between the Potomac and the Temporary Line, and Linton included all that part of the Province west of the Big Tonoloway.

Antietam Hundred was divided in 1758. Elizabeth, Fort Frederick, and Skipton were erected prior to 1775, and Barrens, Morley's Run, Upper Old Town, and Sandy Creek between 1775 and 1785. The present territory of the county was embraced in the following hundreds in 1813: Elizabeth-Town, Lower Antietam, Upper Antietam, Middle Antietam, Jerusalem, Barrens, Sharpsburg, Marsh, Williamsport, Upper Salisbury, Lower Salisbury, Conococheague, Fort Frederick, and Linton. In 1823 the Legislature authorized the levy court to appoint constables for the election districts, and hundreds were no longer recognized as subdivisions of the county.

From the organization of the county in 1776 until 1800 its present territory constituted one election district with the polling place at Hagerstown. In 1800 five election districts were erected. No. 1 (Sharpsburg) included the extreme southeastern part of the county; No. 2 (Williamsport) and No. 3 (Hagerstown) extended from the Conococheague to the South mountain; No. 4 (now Clearspring) was situated between the Potomac and the State line between Nos. 2 and 3 on the east and Green Spring Furnace run on the west; No. 5 (Hancock) included all that part of the county west of No. 4.

District No. 6 (Boonsboro) and No. 7 (Cavetown) were erected in 1822; No. 8 (Rohrersville), in 1833; No. 9 (Leitersburg), in 1838; No. 10 (Funkstown); No. 11 (Sandy Hook) and No. 12 (Tilghmanton), in 1852; No. 13 (Conococheague), in 1858; No. 14 (Ringgold) and No. 15 (Indian Spring), in 1860; No. 16 (Beaver Creek), in 1867; No. 17 (Antietam), in 1869; No. 18 (Chewsville), in 1872; No. 19 (Keedysville), in 1873; No. 20 (Downsville), in 1878; Nos. 21 and 22, in 1884. Three others have since

INTRODUCTION.

been added, two of which are located principally within the corporate limits of Hagerstown; the other is known as Wilson's.

INTERNAL IMPROVEMENTS.

The first road through the Cumberland valley was laid out in 1735-36 from Harris's Ferry on the Susquehanna to the Potomac at the mouth of the Conococheague. Its course through Washington County was nearly identical with the present Williamsport and Greencastle turnpike. Among the county roads in 1749 were the following: "Between the Great Marsh to Potomac and from thence to Conococheague"; "From the Great Marsh to Antietam and from the river to Stull's"; "Up Conococheague to Wolgamot's mill and from thence to the head of the Great Marsh"; "From Baker's to Stull's mill." Under the jurisdiction of the Frederick County court a number of roads were laid out, including many of the most important in the county to-day and some that no longer appear upon the map.

In 1791 a number of important county roads were resurveyed, including the road from Hagerstown to the Frederick County line, from Hagerstown to Hancock, from Hagerstown to Charlton's Gap, from Hagerstown to Nicholson's Gap, from Hagerstown to Williamsport, and from Williamsport to Turner's Gap.

The construction of the Cumberland road was authorized by act of Congress in 1806. Its eastern terminus was at Cumberland, Md., which was connected with Baltimore and Washington by turnpikes constructed by incorporated companies. A great overland highway was thus established from the Atlantic seaboard to the West: It passed through Boonsboro, Hagerstown, and Clearspring and was for many years an important factor in the development and prosperity of the county. A number of other turnpikes have since been constructed.

The Potomac Company was organized in 1785 for the purpose of improving the navigation of that river, the futility of which was finally apparent, and its franchises eventually became vested in the Chesapeake and Ohio Canal Company. The excavation of the canal was begun in 1828, and in 1850 it was completed to Cumberland. It passes through Washington County parallel with the Potomac river.

The construction of the Baltimore and Ohio railroad was begun in 1828; it was opened for travel to Harper's Ferry in 1834 and to Cumberland in 1842. The Washington County branch, which extends from Weverton to Hagerstown, was opened in 1867. The Cumberland Valley railroad was constructed to Hagerstown in 1841 and extended to Martinsburg in 1874. The Western Maryland railroad was opened to Hagerstown in 1872 and to Williamsport in 1873; a lateral line extends from Edgemont to Shippensburg and a western extension from Williamsport to Cherry Run. The Norfolk and Western railroad was opened from Hagerstown to the valley of Virginia in 1880. The street railway system of Hagerstown was constructed in 1896 and is operated by electricity. Lateral lines extend to Williamsport and Funkstown.

Town and Village Growth.

Hagerstown, the county seat of Washington County, was founded in 1762 by Jonathan Hager. The proprietor conferred upon it the name of Elizabeth-Town in honor of his wife, and many years elapsed before the present designation acquired undisputed currency. Rev. Philip V. Fithian, a Presbyterian clergyman, visited Hagerstown on the 18th of May, 1775, and entered the following brief description in his journal:

Hagerstown—a considerable village. It may contain two hundred houses. Some of them are large and neat, built with stone or brick, but the greater part of the houses are built with logs, neatly squared, which indeed make a good house. There are many stores here and many mechanics, and it is a place of business. The inhabitants are chiefly Dutch. East and southeast of this town the Blue mountains appear like thick, hazy thunder clouds just above the horizon in summer. There is here a Dutch Lutheran church and they are building an English church.*

Business and industrial activity has continued to be the prominent characteristic of Hagerstown. Turnpikes and public roads radiate to every part of the county, while its railroad facilities are unsurpassed by those of any other inland city on the Atlantic seaboard.

Sharpsburg received its name in compliment to Horatio Sharpe, Governor of Maryland. It was founded in 1763 by Joseph Chapline, rapidly attained the proportions of a frontier village, and in

---

*Egle's Notes and Queries 1881, p. 156.

1765 its population was deemed sufficient to warrant the appointment of a constable by the Frederick County court. Within a few years after its founding it had become the business center of the lower Antietam valley, and in 1776 it was an unsuccessful aspirant for the location of the county seat. On the 17th of September, 1862, the town and adjacent country were the scene of one of the most important battles of the American Civil War.

Williamsport is situated on the Potomac river at the mouth of the Conococheague. It was founded by General Otho Holland Williams, an officer in the Revolutionary War, and was laid out in 1787 under authority of the Maryland Legislature. The Potomac was then extensively used for the shipment of grain and merchandise, for which Williamsport possessed every advantage as a point of consignment, while the construction of the canal and of the turnpikes to Greencastle and Hagerstown were additional factors in its business growth.

Boonsboro is located at the foot of the South mountain, on the turnpike from Frederick to Hagerstown. A century ago the site of the village was owned by two brothers, George and William Boone, from whom its name is derived. In 1796 it comprised five houses. It received an important impetus from the completion of the turnpike in 1810, and was for many years one of the most important business centers of the county; but with the decline of travel over this thoroughfare its prosperity also suffered, and for some years it has been practically stationary.

Funkstown derives its name from Jacob Funk. Here he built a mill prior to 1768, and before the Revolution he founded the town, of which the original name was Jerusalem. Since the early part of the present century the town has been a manufacturing point of local importance. It is situated on the Boonsboro turnpike, two miles from Hagerstown, with which it is connected by an electric railway.

Hancock, one of the oldest towns in the county, perpetuates the name of its founder, and came into existence prior to 1790. It is situated in the extreme western part of the county on the line of the canal and the old National road.

Smithsburg was founded prior to 1815 by Christopher Smith. It is situated on the Western Maryland railroad at the foot of the South mountain.

Clearspring was founded in 1821 by Martin Myers, who describes it as located "on the turnpike leading from Baltimore to the western country," eleven and one-half miles from Hagerstown and one mile east of the North mountain. It is the business center of a rich agricultural region.

Among the minor villages of the county are Cavetown, Rohrersville, Leitersburg, Chewsville, Tilghmanton, Sandy Hook, Maugansville, etc.

HISTORY OF LEITERSBURG DISTRICT

CHAPTER I.

Early Land Tenure and Settlement.

Antietam — Prehistoric Remains — Longmeadows — Skipton-on-Craven — Deceit — Darling's Sale — Lambert's Park — Downing's Lot — Chester — Well Taught — Allamangle — All That's Left — Rich Barrens — Perry's Retirement — Huckleberry Hall — Dry Spring — Burkhart's Lot — Scant Timber — Father's Good Will — Elysian Fields — The Farmer's Blessing — Addition to Cumberland — Turkey Buzzard — Cumberland — Smaller Tracts — Adjustment of Boundaries — Mason and Dixon's Line.

The watershed of Antietam creek includes the whole of Leitersburg District. A short distance north of the State line two branches of nearly equal volume unite to form this stream, but its only affluent of importance in the District is the Little Antietam, whose waters it receives half a mile below the village of Leitersburg. A smaller stream, known at the beginning of the century as Tipton's run, empties into the Little Antietam near the eastern boundary of the District. Marsh run, which drains the western part of its territory, rises in Franklin County, Pa., where its course possesses political significance for some miles as the boundary of Washington and Antrim Townships. It is also a tributary of the Antietam.

While the name Antietam is perhaps the most enduring memorial of the Indian occupation, there are also others. A well defined village site has been identified a short distance beyond the eastern line of the District at a spring on the farm of C. L. G. Anderson on the north side of Little Antietam. Here hundreds of arrow heads and numerous axes, scrapers, celts, pestles, etc. have been found. In 1831 Ira Hill of Funkstown, Md., published a book entitled "Antiquities of America Explained," in which the following description of prehistoric remains near Leitersburg occurs:

In this part of the extensive valley west of the Blue Ridge are many remains of antiquity. * * * * On the banks of the Antietam near Leitersburg are many such remains. There are numerous arrows of different sizes, many remains of burned bones, large pieces of purest flint of various shapes, and many other kinds of stone curiously carved as if designed for some important use.

There are innumerable pieces of a kind of ware which was undoubtedly manufactured at this place. From the convex and concave surfaces of the pieces it is evident that the vessels were of as many sizes as those made use of at the present time by the generality of community. This ware is about as thick as that generally made in our potteries, and though it may have remained for thousands of years under the earth or exposed on its surface to wind and weather, yet it is harder than any I have ever seen manufactured in any part of the country. The outside is rough as if fashioned into innumerable figures; the inside is as smooth as glass. The rims are likewise adorned with many cuts or figures. The greatest degree of heat that I have been able to apply to this ware seems to have no effect, and other methods I have taken to dissolve it have proved as ineffectual. This ware and many other remains are all mingled together, and among which are to be seen ashes and charcoal. The gentleman on whose ground most of these remains are found observed that when he first ploughed up this field it seemed that bones had been burned in log heaps.

Near to these curiosities on a beautiful bottom are two circles, the one about ten yards in diameter and the other somewhat less. These are in a meadow and though the ground has been cultivated for many years and is on a perfect level with the circles, yet from the growth and color of the grass that grows upon them they are distinctly seen from the surrounding meadow. The soil appears the same as that around them and the whole has been richly manured, yet the grass on these circles has a more thrifty growth than the other. Here were undoubtedly the places on which they moulded their ware or on which they mixed the materials of which it was composed.

Not many hundred yards from these places are many Indian graves; these mounds are still a number of feet higher than the ground around them. A number of gentlemen assisted me in opening one. On account of a mill-dam which has raised the water above the level of the bottom on which these graves were made the water rushed in so fast that we could not succeed entirely to our wishes in this work. But we found pieces of the ware above mentioned, a number of curious stones, and what was once undoubtedly part of a human foot now petrified. These were all incased in a black mud, interspersed with whitish veins, which we conjectured were the remains of bones.

The earliest authentic information regarding the settlement of Leitersburg District is that which occurs in connection with

EARLY LAND TENURE AND SETTLEMENT.

its original land tenure. From this source it is ascertained that there were settlers here prior to 1738. The frontier population of Maryland at that date, like that of the other Atlantic colonies, was composed of a variety of elements. Here the restraints of civilized society were comparatively weak; wants were few and easy of gratification; the cheapness of the land and its certain appreciation in value presented strong inducements for its acquisition. Hence the less ambitious and industrious, the indolent, the shiftless, and the criminal, as well as the adventurous and enterprising, gravitated from the older communities to the frontier. All these classes were doubtless represented in the early population of Leitersburg District. Some of the earliest residents were hunters and trappers rather than agriculturists, mere squatters upon the land they occupied with but little desire for its permanent possession, and their history is as destitute of memorials as that of the savages who preceded them. Then there were others who acquired land and improved it, founded homes and reared families, established churches and schools and the miscellaneous industries of an agricultural community, and laid the foundations of the present social and material development of the District. It is with the latter class and their descendants and successors that these pages are principally concerned.

LONGMEADOWS.

The first tract in Leitersburg District secured by original patent was Longmeadows, which first received this designation in 1738. On the 10th of March in that year Thomas Cresap petitioned the Land Commissioner of the Province for the survey of a tract under this name, for which he received a patent, June 16, 1739. The preamble to the latter instrument recites that "pursuant to our instructions to our Governor and judge in land affairs for granting our back lands on the borders of the Province aforesaid a certain John Church obtained from his Excellency Samuel Ogle, Esq., an order for three hundred acres of vacant land, all whose right, title, and interest of, in, and to the said order and the land therein mentioned the said Church assigned and made over to the petitioner [Cresap]; and forasmuch as he has discovered that quantity of vacant land lying and being in the county aforesaid on one of the branches of Antietam, between that and Conococheague, and near some ponds of fresh water in said Antietam, partly cultivated," a warrant for its survey was issued in his favor, March 10, 1738. This was executed by J. P. Dent, deputy surveyor of Prince George's County, June 14, 1739, and his return describes the boundaries as "Beginning at a bounded red oak, standing on the west side of Neal's meadow, below the mouth of a drain that comes out of a great pond being in the said land." The area of the tract was 550 acres.

Colonel Cresap resided at Longmeadows from 1738 to 1741. The improvements he erected here included a stone building in which he resided and which also served the purposes of a fortification and trading post. It stood on the east bank of Marsh run, on the farm now owned by Mrs. William S. Young, and was doubtless at the time of its erection the most substantial building in Leitersburg District.

The original area of Longmeadows was twice enlarged by Colonel Cresap—July 30, 1742, by an additon of 110 acres, and August 8, 1743, by an addition of one hundred acres. Daniel Dulany secured the entire tract, aggregating 760 acres, in 1746. Within a few years he had it resurveyed, resulting in the acquisition of 1,371 acres of vacant land, thus increasing the area to 2,131 acres, for which he secured a patent, November 7, 1751. In the following year he was granted a warrant for a second resurvey, by which 2,370 acres were added, but owing to disputes with other claimants no patent was issued. He sold the tract to Colonel Henry Bouquet, a native of Switzerland and a British officer of distinction in the French and Indian War, who, "being willing and desirous to adjust the said disputes," secured a second resurvey, as the result of which the area of the tract was increased to 4,163 acres, for which he was granted a patent, September 16, 1763.

Bouquet made the following disposition of Longmeadows by his will, executed on the 25th of June, 1765:

> I constitute and appoint my friend. Colonel Frederick Haldimand, my heir and executor, and to him I give and bequeath all and everything which I may die possessed of in North America, without any exception whatever, upon the condition of paying my just debts and above legacies: my estate, consisting for the present in the farm called Long Meadows Enlarged, situate in Frederick County in the Province of Maryland, * * * the said farm to be sold with

the saw-mill, tan-yard, houses, tenements, and appurtenances on the same for the payment of my debts and legacies.*

It does not appear that Bouquet ever remained at Longmeadows any length of time, although it is not improbable that he designed to make it the place of his residence in the event of his retirement from the army.

Colonel Haldimand was a compatriot of Bouquet. His early military experience was obtained on the Continent, where, like Bouquet, he had been in the service of the Dutch against the French. He entered the British army with the same rank as Bouquet, that of colonel in the Royal American Brigade. The Longmeadows estate continued in his possession until November 6, 1773, when he sold it to Joseph Sprigg of Prince George's County, Md. It is not probable that he ever resided here, although in some legal documents relating to this locality Longmeadows is referred to as "Colonel Haldimand's plantation." In the deed of conveyance to Sprigg he is described as "Frederick Haldimand, at present of the City of New York in the Province of New York, and major general in His Majesty's army."

The Longmeadows tract extended along the western boundary of Leitersburg District from Paradise school house almost to the Pennsylvania line. A considerable part of its area was also beyond the District line on the west and south. It embraced one of the most fertile and desirable sections of Washington County. Fortunately for the development of the District Joseph Sprigg was the last individual owner of this extensive tract, the disintegration of which began about the close of the Revolutionary War. In 1779 he sold to Samuel Hughes 1,300 acres, to John McConkey 521 acres, and to Dr. Henry Schnebley 322 acres, and in the following year 781 acres to Thomas Sprigg.

The purchase of Samuel Hughes embraced the original Longmeadows tract and improvements. In 1789 he sold the entire tract of 1,300 acres to Thomas Hart, who came to Hagerstown in 1780 from Hillsboro, N. C., a locality that he was obliged to leave on account of the depredations of his Tory neighbors. At Hagerstown he engaged in merchandising and was for some years the partner of Nathaniel Rochester, the founder of Rochester, N. Y. He resided at Longmeadows for a time and here a daugh-

---

*Colonel Henry Bouquet and his Campaigns of 1763 and 1764, by Rev. Cyrus Cort, p 76.

ter was born, who afterward became the wife of Henry Clay, the Whig candidate for President in 1844. Hart removed to Kentucky in 1794.

Thomas B. Hall succeeded Colonel Hart in the ownership of 510 acres of the Longmeadows tract, now embraced principally in the farms of Mrs. William S. Young and Abraham Lehman. Hall was connected with the internal revenue service of the United States as collector of direct taxes for the Eighth district of Maryland. There was a deficit of $17,916.68 in his accounts for the years 1815-16, for the recovery of which the United States marshal levied upon the Longmeadows farm; it was sold at public sale, March 30, 1827, and purchased for the United States, to which the marshal accordingly executed a deed, February 15, 1831. From this circumstance it was long known as "the United States farm," and such in fact it was. In 1831 Richard Ragan and William D. Magill, of Hagerstown, purchased it from Virgil Maxey, solicitor of the Treasury of the United States, by deeds "signed, sealed, and delivered in the presence of J. Marshall, Joseph Story," chief justice and associate justice, respectively, of the Supreme Court of the United States. The part purchased by Ragan is now owned by Mrs. William S. Young of Baltimore and that purchased by Magill by Abraham Lehman.

The large brick mansion near the terminus of the Marsh turnpike was built by Thomas Sprigg, whose purchase of 781 acres from the Longmeadows tract has been mentioned. His estate eventually comprised 1,754 acres and bore the name of Sprigg's Paradise. It consisted of 1,581 acres from Longmeadows Enlarged, Pleasant Spring (seventy-eight acres, patented by John Rench in 1760), Race Ground (twelve acres, patented by Joseph Sprigg in 1776), and The Grove (eighty-five acres, patented by Joseph Sprigg in 1777). General Sprigg secured a warrant for the resurvey of these tracts in 1785, but the patent was not issued until December 12, 1804. Sprigg's Paradise was situated on both sides of the Marsh turnpike. The proprietor, who was a member of Congress, brigadier general in the State militia, and otherwise prominent in public affairs, resided here until his death in 1809, and in 1810 the estate was divided among his three children. The Sprigg residence and several hundred acres adjacent thereto are now owned by the Messrs. Cressler.

In 1780 McConkey sold the land he had purchased from Joseph

Sprigg to John Rench, whose son, Peter Rench, resided thereon; in 1833 the larger part of this tract was purchased from his heirs by Jacob B. Lehman.

In 1789 Thomas Hart sold to John Dorsett six hundred acres of land, of which 395 acres were purchased from Dorsett by Wendell Gilbert in 1791. Samuel Gilbert, his son, subsequently owned part of this land, which embraced the Paradise spring and the site of Longmeadows church.

SKIPTON-ON-CRAVEN.

Colonel Cresap was also the owner of an original tract several miles east of Longmeadows, and to this he gave the name of Skipton-on-Craven, his native place in England. The certificate of survey, returned under date of November 27, 1740, describes the boundaries as "Beginning at a bounded Spanish oak standing on the south side of a branch of Antietam known by the name of Forbush's branch;" and in the preamble to the patent, which was granted March 27, 1744, the tract is described as "lying and being in the County aforesaid in the fork of Antietam creek, whereon a certain Thomas Catens formerly settled and made some improvements."

In 1749 "Michael Miller, yeoman, of Frederick County," purchased Skipton-on-Craven from Colonel Cresap. Nothing is known regarding his personal history, although it may be stated with certainty that he resided for many years in the vicinity of Leitersburg near the mouth of Little Antietam. Here he owned at one time about seven hundred acres of land, now embraced in the Ziegler, Hartle, and Stockslager farms. In 1760 he was constable for Upper Antietam Hundred.

In 1765 John Reiff purchased from Michael Miller 117 acres of land, part of Skipton-on-Craven, "whereon John Reiff now lives." He was therefore an actual resident of the District and a near neighbor to Jacob Leiter. By successive purchases he eventually acquired more than four hundred acres of land, southwest of Leitersburg and on both sides of the Antietam and the turnpike, much of which was doubtless reduced to cultivation and improved by him.

Jacob Good was also a resident of the District as early as 1765, when he purchased from Michael Miller 163 acres, part of

Skipton-on-Craven, "being the land whereon the said Good now lives." Good's house was a log building and stood between the Little Antietam and the stone residence of Harvey J. Hartle. It was near the bank of the creek, and on the opposite side there was a saw-mill. Surrounding these improvements Good owned 350 acres of land, embracing the confluence of Antietam and Little Antietam, the whole of Harvey J. Hartle's farm, and adjacent lands now owned by Levi Hartle, John Hartle, and Alveh L. Stockslager. In 1787 he sold this land to Joseph Long, his son-in-law, from whom in 1795 it passed to John Barr, of Lancaster County, Pa.

In 1775 Christian Lantz, formerly a resident of Lancaster County, Pa., purchased from John Reiff 476 acres of land southwest of Leitersburg, along the turnpike and Antietam creek. Here he resided until his death in 1798. In 1776 he was a member of the County Committee of Safety. A large part of his landed estate is still in possession of his descendants. He built one of the first mills in the District.

Deceit.

"Forbush's branch" is now known as Little Antietam, the latter designation having completely superseded the former, which would no longer be recognized in this locality. Yet George Forbush, from whom the stream derived the name by which it was known in 1740, was undoubtedly one of the earliest settlers along its course; and although he took his departure about the time the first permanent settlers began to arrive, the location of his plantation can be determined with a fair degree of probability. On the 23d of August, 1743, John Darling secured a patent for Deceit, a tract of 108 acres, the boundaries of which are described as "Beginning at a bounded white oak standing nigh a branch of Antietam on the top of a steep hill and near the place that George Forbush formerly lived on." In the patent for Darling's Sale (surveyed in 1739), its boundaries are described as "Beginning at a bounded white oak standing on the southeast side of Little Antietam creek, near the plantation of one George Forbush." From a plot of the Stoner lands entered in the land records of Washington County in 1820, it is ascertained that this "bounded white oak" stood on the present line between the lands of Daniel W.

EARLY LAND TENURE AND SETTLEMENT.

Durboraw and Charles B. and Levi B. Wolfinger; the "steep hill" referred to in the patent for Deceit is therefore embraced principally in the property of Jacob B. Stoner and the Forbush plantation doubtless included the adjacent meadows.

Joseph Perry purchased Deceit from John Darling in 1754. He secured a resurvey thereon, whereby its area was increased to 658 acres; the patent was issued on the 17th of February, 1761, and the tract received the name of The Resurvey on Deceit. It embraced, wholly or in part, the farms of Oliver F. Lantz, William H. Stevenson, Charles B. and Levi B. Wolfinger, C. L. G. Anderson, Jacob B. Stoner, Mrs. Elizabeth Stoner, and others. This extensive tract continued in Perry's possession until 1779, when he sold it to Daniel Hughes, from whom it was purchased by Benjamin and John Crockett of Baltimore. In 1783 they sold it to Martin Barr, of Lancaster County, Pa., by whom the improvements on the Anderson farm, the mill, etc., were built. In 1801 he sold 193 acres to John Stoner and in 1823 Daniel Winter purchased from Colonel John Barr 310 acres, embracing the Anderson and Lantz farms, etc.

DARLING'S SALE.

Captain John Charlton was a contemporary of Forbush. His principal landed estate in Leitersburg District was the tract called Darling's Sale, which he purchased from John Darling, by whom its acquisition from the Proprietaries was initiated. The survey in Captain Charlton's favor was returned under date of February 1, 1739, and describes the tract as bounded by a line "Beginning at a bounded white oak standing on the southeast side of Little Antietam creek, near the plantation of one George Forbush." The patent was issued on the 14th of October, 1743. The area of the tract was 420 acres. It was situated in the vicinity of Martin's school house and is now embraced in the farms of Daniel Durboraw, Curtis Fogler, John B. Newcomer, and others. After Captain Charlton's death it was divided into seven tracts of sixty acres each, which were apportioned by lot among his children.

In 1792 lots Nos. 4 and 6 became the subject of litigation. It was claimed by Richard Right that Thomas Charlton had leased to him for a term of ten years "part of a tract of land called Darling's Sale, known and distinguished by lot No. 4, containing sixty acres of land, forty whereof is arable land and twenty acres of woodland, and one other part of said tract of land called Darling's Sale, known and distinguished by lot No. 6, containing in the whole sixty acres of land, forty-five whereof is arable land and fifteen in meadow, and also * * * two dwelling houses, a barn, and malt-kiln," from which he was ejected by Poynton Charlton. For this he entered suit for damages; the case was tried at April term, 1794, resulting adversely to the plaintiff. Captain Charlton's descendants are still residents of Washington County, although the family name long since ceased to be familiar in the locality where its first representative settled more than a century and a half ago.

Lambert's Park.

George Lambert was also an early settler in close proximity to Forbush and Charlton. On the 18th of November, 1742, he secured a patent for two hundred acres of land under the name of Lambert's Park, the boundaries of which are described as "Beginning at a bounded white oak standing on the north side of a branch of Antietam near the mouth of a run that comes from Captain Charlton's and falls into the aforesaid branch." This tract is partly embraced in the lands of Joseph Martin, the heirs of Jacob E. Bell, and John Wishard. Lambert was also the original owner of several other tracts in this vicinity. His direct descendants resided in the District for several generations and are still represented at Hagerstown.

Downing's Lot.

A short distance south of the present District line near the Hagerstown and Waynesboro turnpike stands a substantial stone house on the farm of Daniel N. Scheller inscribed in one of the gables with the date 1750. Here Robert Downing resided until his death in 1755. He had a hundred acres of land surveyed here in 1739, but his first acquisition appears to have been a tract of fifty acres, Downing's Lot, surveyed on the 1st of October, 1742, with a boundary "Beginning at a bounded walnut standing in a glade about a quarter of a mile from the said Downing's house." The patent was issued on the 13th of July, 1743. In the following year the tract was resurveyed and its area was increased to

319 acres. In the return of this survey the "beginning tree" is described as "standing in the marsh that leads from Captain Thomas Cresap's to Antietam creek." A second resurvey was made in 1754, by which the tract attained an area of 754 acres; the patent was granted on the 4th of April, 1755. It extended from the turnpike to Antietam creek at Trovinger's mill and embraced the site of Antietam church, one of the earliest places of worship in Washington County.

CHESTER.

Robert Downing was also the original owner of Chester, a tract of one hundred acres, for which he was granted a patent on the 23d of August, 1744. Its boundary began "at a bounded black oak tree standing on the east side of Antietam about a mile and a half below the sugar bottom"—evidently the same sugar bottom referred to in the survey of Neal's Bottom (1747). In 1752 it was resurveyed and enlarged to 388 acres. This tract includes the lands of Simon Clopper and others in the southern part of the District.

WELL TAUGHT.

George Poe was another of the pioneers of the District of whom but little is known beyond his name and the fact of his residence here. On the 10th of February, 1748, he secured a warrant for the survey of one hundred acres of land, the return of which was certified to the land office under date of July 4, 1749, and on the same day a patent was issued in his favor. The tract received the name of Well Taught and its boundaries are described as "Beginning at a bounded white oak standing on the east side of Antietam near the creek and over against the said Poe's plantation." It is difficult to identify the site of Poe's plantation. Well Taught was subsequently embraced in Rich Barrens, an original tract patented to Peter Shiess; it was also adjacent to the Antietam on the west side and the only farms adjacent to the Antietam into which Rich Barrens enters are those formerly owned by Joseph and William Gabby and now by Hiram D. Middlekauff and the heirs of the late Joseph Strite. Here there are extensive meadows on the west side of the creek, and there can be little doubt that George Poe resided there in 1749.

The Resurvey on Well Taught.

After Poe had resided here about four years he conceived the design of extending his landed possessions—a procedure by no means unusual at the period when large tracts were secured and held solely for speculative purposes and the only limit to individual acquisition was the ability to pay the nominal price required by the provincial authorities. Accordingly, on the 16th of March, 1752, he secured a warrant for the survey of "some vacant land" that he had discovered contiguous to Well Taught. Not having been executed within the time required the warrant was renewed on the 28th of August following, in pursuance of which twelve hundred acres of vacant land were added and the tract received the name of The Resurvey on Well Taught, with a total area of thirteen hundred acres. The patent was issued on the 14th of March, 1754. This tract embraced the site of Leitersburg; its principal extent was east and southeast of the village, although it also extended north as far as the mill that formerly stood on the land of Samuel Martin.

That Poe secured this extensive tract for speculative purposes is shown by the fact that in the following year he disposed of eight hundred acres, nearly two-thirds of its area. The respective purchasers were Michael Miller, 409 acres; William Hall, 115 acres; Michael Leatherman, 52 acres; Robert Hartness, 51 acres, and Christopher Burkhart, 173 acres; to all of whom deeds were executed on the 17th of March, 1755. Of The Resurvey on Well Taught the original owner eventually retained 362 acres, but before disposing of this he initiated proceedings for a second resurvey. The first resurvey was principally east of the Antietam; west of that creek he discovered an extensive tract of vacant land, for the survey of which he secured a warrant in 1761, but before completing the title he sold his landed interests here to Jacob Leiter. About this time he purchased land on Fishing creek in Frederick County, in which at a later date there was a a large connection of Poes near the town of Jefferson, although the family is no longer represented there.

George Hartle was a resident of Leitersburg District in 1760 and perhaps earlier; it was in 1760 that he purchased from Leatherman the fifty-two acres the latter had bought from Poe in

1755. By the acquisition of several original tracts and the purchase of others he owned at his death in 1776 350 acres of land, now embraced in the farms of Samuel Hartle, Henry and Frederick Hartle, and Alveh L. Stockslager. It is believed that he built and occupied the present dwelling house on the farm of Samuel Hartle. His descendants are more numerous in the District today than those of any other of its pioneer settlers.

In 1797 Jacob Miller purchased 162 acres of land, now embraced in the farm of Samuel Hartle, part of which was formerly owned by Martin Hartle and constituted his part of his father's estate. Here Jacob Miller lived until his death in 1822. His son, Jacob Miller, from whom Miller's church derived its name, was born and reared here.

THE RESURVEY ON POE'S PART OF WELL TAUGHT.

In 1762 Jacob Leiter became a resident of the locality that perpetuates his family name. From George Poe he purchased 362 acres of land, embracing the site of Leitersburg, the Barkdoll and Summer farms, etc., and here he resided until his death two years later. It is not improbable that the oldest part of the present house on the farm of Joseph Barkdoll was built and occupied by him. Poe also assigned to Leiter his interest in a resurvey on Well Taught then pending; Leiter completed the title and secured a patent, which was issued in his favor, April 19, 1763. Nearly a thousand acres of vacant land were added, increasing the area of the tract to 1,294 acres. It was called The Resurvey on Poe's Part of Well Taught, and embraced some of the finest farms in the central part of the District, including, wholly or in part, those of the late David and Joseph Strite, Henry L. Strite, Noah E. Shank, William H. Kreps, John F. Strite, W. Harvey Hykes, Mrs. Mary A. Hykes, Henry M. Jacobs, John C. Miller, Edward M. White, and others.

Previous to his death Jacob Leiter had arranged for the sale of nearly a thousand acres of The Second Resurvey on Well Taught, and in his will he gave the following instructions to his executors: "I empower my executors to convey to the several [parties] hereafter named all that tract of land which was assigned to me by George Poe according to the agreement and compact between the parties, viz., to Christian Leiter, Jacob Good,

John Reiff, Jacob Ritter, Philip Reinall, and to Henry Fore." Accordingly, in October, 1765, Andrew Hoover and John Reiff, the executors referred to, deeded to Christian Leiter 107 acres, to Jacob Good 145, to John Reiff 144, to Jacob Ritter 216, to Philip Reinall 119, and to Henry Fore 233. Another clause of Jacob Leiter's will read as follows: "I give and bequeath unto my two youngest sons, Jacob Leiter and Peter Leiter, the place of land whereon I now live, containing 362 acres more or less." Thus the extensive landed estate of the testator was divided among nearly a dozen individuals the year after his death.

Christian Leiter's land was northwest of Leitersburg on the Greencastle road. In 1793 he sold it to Michael Wolfinger, a native of Germany, who located here and was engaged in farming, distilling, blacksmithing, and hotel-keeping until his death in 1816. He has numerous descendants in the District.

Jacob Ritter's part of the Leiter lands is now embraced principally in the farms of Henry M. Jacobs and Mrs. Mary A. Hykes. On the line between these two farms is a well, referred to in old deeds as "Jacob Ritter's well." The line of division was run across the well in order that the occupants of both farms might have access to it. Here Jacob Ritter resided until his death in 1804.

Henry Fore's purchase of 233 acres was embraced in Collier's Amendment, a tract of 448 acres granted by patent to Frederick Nicodemus, October 8, 1768. In 1779 Nicodemus also purchased Reinall's part of the Leiter lands.

ALLAMANGLE.

Peter Shiess was an extensive land owner in Leitersburg District at the period to which this chapter relates. His first acquisition was Allamangle, a tract of one hundred acres, for which he secured a warrant, August 22, 1750. The boundaries are described as "Beginning at a bounded wild cherry tree near a marked rock about three poles from Antietam creek on the west side thereof." This tract is principally embraced in the farm of Lewis Lecron, although it also included the channel of the creek for some distance above the mill that formerly stood on the land of Samuel Martin. In the patent, which was granted October 9, 1752, Shiess is described as "a German Protestant." There can

EARLY LAND TENURE AND SETTLEMENT.

be little doubt that he became a resident of the District at this time, as he is known to have resided here for many years.

ALL THAT'S LEFT.

The area of this tract was 597 acres; it was granted to Peter Shiess by original patent, May 4, 1765, and adjoined The Resurvey on Well Taught. In 1767 two brothers, Peter and Anthony Bell, purchased land from Shiess, the former 248 acres, the latter 105 acres, parts of All That's Left. Peter Bell's land is embraced principally in the farms of Joseph M. Bell and Daniel S. Wolfinger; Anthony Bell's, in that of the heirs of John Eshleman. Anthony Bell resided here until his death in 1812; Peter Bell died at Hagerstown in 1778. He was a member of the County Committee of Safety in 1776.

RICH BARRENS.

The most extensive tract acquired by Peter Shiess was Rich Barrens, the area of which was 1,154 acres. The warrant for its survey was issued on the 4th of May, 1765; the patent, April 27, 1767. The preamble to the latter instrument states that he "was seized in fee of and in a tract or parcel of land called Well Taught, * * * originally on the 4th day of July, A. D. 1749, granted unto a certain George Poe for one hundred acres," contiguous to which he had discovered some vacant land, etc. Rich Barrens included, wholly or in part, the farms owned by Mrs. Abraham Strite, the heirs of Joseph Strite, John S. Strite, Franklin M. Strite, Daniel Hoover, Mrs. Martha H. Leiter, Daniel W. Martin, and others; it also extended into Pennsylvania, where it enters into the farms of Henry Barkdoll, Upton W. Harshman, and Joseph Shank.

In 1770 Shiess sold 713 acres to Dr. Henry Schnebley, who gave to his purchase the name of The Forest. Several years later he sold two hundred acres to Philip Boyer, from whom it was purchased by Daniel Mowen; in 1777 this land was bought by Henry Schriver, who located thereon in August of that year. It was part of the agreement between them "that the said Daniel Mowen and family have free privilege to live in the dwelling house on said premises with the said Henry Schriver and family, and likewise enjoy the full use of his own property and equal share of stabling for and until the 1st day of April, which shall be in the year of our Lord 1778, the summer crops, viz., oats, corn, and hay, to be divided between the said parties hereunto, share and share alike." Three generations of Schrivers, each bearing the surname of Henry, successively resided upon the land thus purchased. It is now embraced principally in the farm of Mrs. Martha H. Leiter.

Dr. Schnebley sold 142 acres to Abraham Leiter in 1774, reserving "liberty to himself or any other person whatsoever, they, their heirs, or assigns forever to have liberty and a free passage to go and carry water of and from the spring or well now situated in the above mentioned land sold by the above Henry Schnebley, Sr., to the above named Abraham Leiter whatever is useful and necessary for the people that live at present or any other people that possess the land whereon Philip Boyer now lives on thenceforth forever; providing always that they all every one of them do no other damage or hurt to said Abraham Leiter's land and to said spring or well than carry off water for the use of their family and cattle in the summer time or when the water is low and do not run that they may have recourse by a path to said spring or well." This reservation shows the importance attached to running water. The well referred to is situated on the farm of Franklin M. Strite, which embraces a large part of the land sold by Schnebley to Leiter. The latter sold it in 1782 to Melchoir Beltzhoover from whom it was purchased in 1792 by Henry Schriver, who devised it by will to his son John. Among the subsequent owners were George Shiess, Frederick Bell, John Horst, and Henry Funk.

That part of The Forest between the Schriver farms and Jacobs church was sold in 1800 by Dr. Schnebley to Albertus Hafner, who had probably resided thereon as tenant for some years previously. John Simpson owned this land from 1809 to 1814, when he sold it to Samuel Garver, who resided there until 1832; he then removed to Greene Township, Franklin County, Pa., where his descendants now live. This land is now owned by Daniel Hoover.

Perry's Retirement.

Joseph Perry was also the original owner of a tract of one hundred acres near Leitersburg, to which he gave the name of Perry's

EARLY LAND TENURE AND SETTLEMENT.

Retirement. The patent was granted on the 29th of September, 1755. In the following year he sold this tract to William Hall and Robert Hartness in equal parts. In 1762 Hall sold 166 acres (116 from The Resurvey on Well Taught and fifty from Perry's Retirement) to Jacob Leiter, who devised it by will to Peter Good, the husband of his daughter Anna, from whom it was purchased in 1769 by John Gabby. He resided here for a number of years and eventually acquired a landed estate of several hundred acres, which was subsequently owned by his sons, William and Joseph. The Gabby lands are now owned by Hiram D. Middlekauff, John A. Bell, C. C. Hollinger, and the estate of the late Joseph Strite.

HUCKLEBERRY HALL.

Huckleberry Hall was originally surveyed for Daniel Dulany, December 5, 1742, but before completing the title he died. The patent was granted to Jacob French, September 29, 1759; its area was one hundred acres, the boundary of which was described as "Beginning at a bounded white oak standing by the side of Forbush's branch, a draught of Antietam creek." The next owner was John Schnebley, from whom this tract with other adjacent land aggregating 240 acres was leased by Jacob Good in 1770. It was specified that at the expiration of the lease "There will be left with the place all buildings such as it is at present, with all the improvements; likewise the table and benches in the house; also two bedsteads, with divers household goods, the iron stove excepted." The value of all "building, clearing, ditching, or damming the water" done by Good was to be appraised by four men. In 1772 he purchased the entire tract. Here he resided from 1787 until his death in 1797. Huckleberry Hall was subsequently owned by the Barrs and Winters and is now embraced partly in the farm of C. L. G. Anderson.

DRY SPRING.

Frederick Fogler was the original owner of Dry Spring, a tract of 129 acres principally embraced in the farm of John S. Strite near New Harmony school. His patent was granted on the 26th of August, 1762. That he actually resided here is shown by a deed executed in his favor in 1770 by Peter Shiess for fifty-three acres, part of Rich Barrens, the boundary of which is described as "Beginning at the beginning tree of a tract of land called Dry Spring, being the land whereon the said Frederick Fogler now lives." The "dry spring" has been identified as a shallow well near Mr. Strite's house, and in all probability Fogler's improvements were in the immediate vicinity. He sold this property in 1778 to John Johnson, from whom it was purchased in 1780 by Philip Snell. He resided here until his death in 1789 and devised the property by will to his son Henry, by whom it was sold in 1797 to John Strite, formerly of Lancaster County, Pa., the ancestor of the Strite family of Leitersburg District. It has since continued in possession of his descendants.

BURKHART'S LOT.

Christopher Burkhart has been mentioned as the purchaser of land from George Poe in 1755, the boundary of which is described as "Beginning at the beginning tree of the tract of land the said Burkhart now lives on," which shows that he was a resident of the District at that date. Here he built one of the first mills, the site of which is now marked by the ruins of a similar structure on the property of Samuel Martin. He resided there in 1755, as evidenced by the patent for Hunt for Timber, a tract now embraced in the farm near Rock Forge owned by the heirs of John Eshleman; the original boundary of this tract was surveyed in 1755 and is described as "Beginning at a bounded black oak standing on the north side of a hill on the east side of Great Antietam about one mile above Christopher Burkhart's."

In 1759 Burkhart secured a patent for Neal's Bottom, a tract originally surveyed in 1747, the boundary of which began "at a bounded Spanish oak standing on the hillside on the west side of Antietam * * * two miles above the sugar bottom." This tract, as well as his purchase from Poe, was included in Burkhart's Lot, the area of which was 638 acres; the patent was issued in his favor, September 29, 1764. It embraced, wholly or in part, the lands now owned by Samuel Martin, Benjamin F. Baker, Isaac Needy, Daniel Oller, Joseph Wishard, Mrs. Margaret Leather, C. C. Hollinger, Upton Clopper, Henry Martin, and Immanuel and Kate E. Martin.

That part embraced in the farms of Upton Clopper and Henry

EARLY LAND TENURE AND SETTLEMENT.

Martin was purchased from Burkhart in 1768 by Nicholas Shafer, who sold it in 1785 to Henry Solmes. He resided here until his death in 1799 and left two daughters, Catharine and Margaret. The former married John Mentzer, who received that part of her father's estate embraced in the Martin farm, where he lived until his death; the latter married Andrew Bell, who thus acquired the Clopper farm, and resided thereon until 1834.

In 1765 John Scott purchased sixty-one acres from Burkhart; in 1770 he secured a resurvey thereon with an area of 298 acres, designated in the patent as The Resurvey on Part of Burkhart's Lot. The boundary is described as "Beginning at a bounded white oak standing on the north side of Tipton's run, it being the beginning tree of a tract of land belonging to George Lambert." Tipton's run is the stream that crosses the Smithsburg road near Martin's school house. A part of this resurvey with considerable adjacent land was acquired prior to 1792 by Peter Stotler, who lived near Little Antietam at the present residence of John B. Barkdoll, where he died in 1835. In 1773 the larger part of Scott's resurvey (223 acres) including the site of Bowman's mill, the farms of Immanuel and Kate E. Martin, etc., came into possession of Christian Hyple, who probably resided thereon during the Revolution. After him the successive owners were Abraham Stouffer, Jacob Gilbert, and Abraham Moyer.

A short distance down the creek from Bowman's mill stands a substantial stone house, in one of the gables of which is this inscription: "H. B. Hockman, 1803." This property is now owned by the heirs of the late Henry G. Clopper. Hockman purchased it in 1785 from Casper Swenk and resided here until his death, May 29, 1813. In the deed to Hockman the land is described as part of three original tracts, viz., The Resurvey on Part of Burkhart's Lot, Little Valley, and Chaney's Choice. It is probable that Swenk resided here before Hockman. He purchased Little Valley in 1771 from John Lambert of Augusta County, Va.

After disposing of about two hundred acres from Burkhart's Lot the original owner had the remainder resurveyed under the name of Burkhart's Establishment, for which he was granted a patent on the 11th of April, 1794. Its area was 440 acres, now embraced principally in the lands of Benjamin F. Baker, Samuel Martin, Daniel Oller, Isaac Needy, and Joseph Wishard.

SCANT TIMBER.

Pelican was granted to Andrew Slush, October 27, 1759, with an area of ninety-five acres and adjoined The Resurvey on Chester. Wendell Sights, a subsequent owner, secured a resurvey with an area of 540 acres and changed the name to Scant Timber, for which he was granted a patent on the 10th of March, 1766. This land adjoined the road that leads from the turnpike to the Old Forge, and Sights resided here for some years.

FATHER'S GOOD WILL.

The original name of this tract was Content, patented to John Stoner on the 24th of May, 1762, with an area of 230 acres. He secured a warrant for a resurvey, by which the area was increased to 1,365 acres, but died before completing the title; John Stoner, his oldest son, sold it to David Stoner, to whom the patent was granted, September 1, 1774, under the name of Father's Good Will.

This tract comprised the northeastern part of the District and also extended into Ringgold. It was one of the last of the extensive original grants to be settled and improved. The principal purchasers of the Stoner lands in Leitersburg District were Christian Garver, 197 acres, 1790; John Mentzer, 100 acres, 1793, and 30 acres, 1801; Peter Stotler, 109 acres, 1801. The farm now owned by William H. Hoffman was embraced in Christian Garver's first purchase; his son, Isaac Garver, also resided here and in 1830 it was purchased by Jacob Barr. Garver subsequently bought one hundred acres from Abraham Stoner; it was also part of Father's Good Will and is now included in the farm of Mrs. Mary M. Newcomer. The greater part of the Mentzer land has continued in possession of the family four generations and is now owned by E. Keller Mentzer. Stotler's purchase was devised by will to his daughter Catharine, wife of Henry Yesler, who resided here for some years.

ELYSIAN FIELDS.

Among the original tracts in the extreme northwestern part of the District were Scott's Grief, one hundred acres, patented to Wiliam Douglass, May 4, 1752; Work Easy, twenty acres, patented to Henry Fore, June 10, 1761; The Resurvey on

Nicholas's Contrivance, patented to James Downing, all of which eventually came into possession of Wiliam Douglass together with part of Collier's Amendment. He was a resident here in 1765. On the 27th of May, 1788, his son, Samuel Douglass, secured a warrant for the resurvey of these lands under the name of Elysian Fields, the area of which was 237 acres. In 1794 the tract was purchased from Samuel Douglass by Ignatius Taylor, who resided here until his death in 1807. The subsequent owners were Joseph Sprigg, Daniel Sprigg, Henry Funk, Henry Myers, and Daniel Jacobs, whose purchase was made in 1825. It is now owned principally by his descendants, Isaac Hykes and J. H. Hykes.

The Farmer's Blessing.

The patent for this tract was granted to Dr. Henry Schnebley, November 16, 1793. It was a resurvey on Scant Timber, Schnebley's Neglect, Walker's Welcome to Antietam (forty-eight acres, patented to Samuel Hughes, August 7, 1770), and Well Meant (305 acres, patented to Thomas Johns, September 7, 1770). The original area was 573 acres. Dr. Schnebley died in 1805, having devised this tract to his son, Jacob Schnebley, who resided here for a time. In 1828 it was purchased from the administrators of his estate by Frederick Ziegler, whose descendants still own a considerable part of it.

Addition to Cumberland.

This was a resurvey on All That's Left, Search Well and You Will Find, and Hunt for Timber (one hundred acres, patented to George Keeler, November 24, 1755). The patentee was Anthony Bell; the patent was granted on the 11th of April, 1794, and the area of the tract was two hundred acres. It is situated near Rock Forge and is now owned by the heirs of John Eshleman.

Turkey Buzzard.

This was a tract of 506 acres, a resurvey on Longmeadows Enlarged, Collier's Amendment, and Well Meant. The patent was granted to Thomas Belt, October 24, 1794. In 1827 it was purchased by George I. Harry, who gave it the name of Colebrook. Both Belt and Harry resided here. It is now embraced partly in the farm of Isaac Shank.

CUMBERLAND.

This was originally a tract of one hundred acres, patented to John Stoner, October 13, 1750. Its boundary is described as "Beginning at a small bounded locust about fifty yards north of Antietam creek about two miles from the Temporary Line." In 1791 Daniel Hughes purchased from the heirs of Peter Shiess all of Allamangle, All That's Left, and Rich Barrens not previously sold, and in the same year he applied for a resurvey that should embrace all these lands, together with Cumberland and Great Rocks. Legal obstacles were encountered, however, and the patent was not granted until September 17, 1810. The tract was called Cumberland, and its area was 658 acres. It embraced, wholly or in part, the farms of Leonard Senger, Daniel V. Shank, Lewis Lecron, John Kriner, Mrs. Fanny Strite, and William Barkdoll, extending across the northern central part of the District from near Jacobs church to the Leitersburg and Ringgold road. Colonel Hughes died in 1818, having devised this extensive tract by will to his son Robert, in whose possession it continued until his death in 1829.

SMALLER TRACTS.

In addition to the large tracts described the District also included others of smaller area. For instance, in a deed from Michael Grebill to Sebastian Hartle (1813) for 275 acres adjacent to the road from Leitersburg to Chewsville the following original tracts are mentioned: The Resurvey on Well Taught, Skipton-on-Craven, Good, Hartle's Lot, The Resurvey on Poe's Part of Well Taught, Surveyor's Last Shift, Miller's Fancy, Strawberry Bottom, Small Timber, Jacob, Johnson's Lot, Baker's Rest, and Fry's Lot. And in a deed from Alexander Claggett to John Strite (1817) for 282 acres, now embraced in the farms of John F. Strite and W. Harvey Hykes, Brown's Grief, The Resurvey on Poe's Part of Well Taught, Collier's Amendment, The Resurvey on Well Meant, The Resurvey on Small Gain, and Tom's Chance are mentioned as constituent tracts. Brown's Grief was surveyed in 1753 and patented by John McClelland in 1771. Its area was thirty acres. The boundary began "at a bounded Spanish oak standing on the northwest side of a stony hill near a great marsh known by the name of the black meadow."

Adjustment of Boundaries.

The original tracts were laid out with but little regard to regularity of outline. The prospective purchaser or his agent visited the locality in which he desired to secure land, and having approximately determined the number of acres in the proposed tract applied to the provincial land office for a warrant for its survey, which was executed by a deputy surveyor. Marshes and hills were avoided; smooth land of apparent fertility was most desired, and hence the lines were usually run so as to include as much of the latter and as little of the former as possible, often resulting in an almost interminable succession of courses and distances.

In determining the boundaries of a tract of land it is essential to know with certainty the location of some point from which distance and direction have been taken. The point most desirable for this purpose is "the place of beginning," which in the original surveys was usually a bounded tree; i. e., a notched tree or one from which the bark was removed in a circle a foot or more wide. This served the immediate purpose well enough, but such a tree dies as a result of the process and in the course of years falls to the ground, undistinguishable from others that have shared the same fate. When this occurred it became a matter of importance to identify the point the tree was intended to mark; and in cases of this kind the law provided that on application by the owner of the tract the county court should appoint commissioners to meet upon the ground, take testimony, and erect a permanent corner-stone. Thus, at August session, 1769, upon petition of Lawrence O'Neal, the Frederick County court appointed a commission to determine and perpetuate the boundary of Great Rocks. Two of the commissioners, Daniel Hughes and William Beard, met on the tract in question, June 2, 1770, when the following proceedings were taken:

The boundary, a large white oak, being destroyed, there is set up a stone at the same place marked on the south side G B R.

Peter Bell, being duly sworn, sayeth that a large white oak where the stone marked as above is set up he heard was the boundary of Great Rocks and saw references taken from it by said name.

Anthony Bell, being sworn, saith that he saw a small white oak bush which grew close to the old white oak marked for the boundary of Great Rocks in place of said old tree, and said small bush stands there still but is on the decay; and likewise was sworn chain carrier when reference was taken from said white oak by the name of the boundary of Great Rocks.

Peter Shiess, being sworn, saith as above and no more.

The boundary of Skipton-on-Craven was similarly determined on the 6th of November, 1772, by William Beard and Christopher Burkhart, commissioners appointed by the Frederick County court upon petition of Jacob Good. The proceedings in this case were as follows:

George Hartle, being sworn, saith that he was two times with the surveyors and saw them start from an old Spanish oak, which oak went by the name of the boundary of Skipton-on-Craven, and that for several years he understood said oak to be the boundary of Skipton-on-Craven.

John Reiff solemnly affirmeth and saith that he frequently saw the surveyors run to and from an old Spanish oak near Jacob Good's saw-mill by the name of the boundary of Skipton-on-Craven.

Frederick Hartle, being sworn, saith he was chain carrier when the surveyor ran that part of land called Skipton-on-Craven and that they ran from an old Spanish oak near Jacob Good's saw-mill, which oak he understood was the boundary of Skipton-on-Craven.

George Lambert, being sworn, saith he saw an old Spanish oak near Jacob Good's saw-mill, notched on two sides, and for many years knew it by the name of the boundary of Skipton-on-Craven.

The above boundary being destroyed, we have set up a stone marked on the south side "1772" and three holes marked with a punch, and on the east edge three marks with said punch.

The disappearance of old landmarks and the frequency of disputes over boundary lines resulted in 1786 in the passage of an act of Assembly authorizing the owners of contiguous lands to unite in the employment of a competent surveyor to run the lines of their respective holdings and erect permanent corner-stones. Under the provisions of this law an extensive resurvey was made in 1792, embracing the site of Leitersburg and many farms in the center of the District. The parties to this agreement were John Gabby, Christopher Burkhart, Jacob Leiter, Martin Grider, Christian Lantz, George Lantz, Peter Leiter, Henry Solmes, Samuel Kraumer, Sebastian Hartle, Joseph Long, Frederick Hartle, Henry Walter, and Peter Stotler, and the surveyor was Ambrose Geohagen. Division lines were resurveyed, discrepancies adjusted, conflicting claims compromised, and corner-stones erected, inscribed with the date, 1792, and distinguishing initials. Some of these monuments still possess legal significance, although in the lapse of a hundred years the boundaries of farms have changed.

In 1811 a similar resurvey was made by Jonas Hogmire for a number of land owners in the northeastern part of Leitersburg District and adjacent territory in Ringgold and Cavetown.

Mason and Dixon's Line.

Mason and Dixon's Line, the northern boundary of the District and for many years the northern limit of slavery, represents the conclusion of a controversy continued through several generations between the successive Proprietaries of Maryland and Pennsylvania. By the terms of Lord Baltimore's charter his grant extended northward "unto that part of Delaware Bay which lieth under the fortieth degree of north latitude and westward in a right line." These limits embraced the State of Delaware and a strip of Pennsylvania territory about twenty miles wide, including the city of Philadelphia. The southern limit of Penn's grant is described as "a circle drawn at twelve miles distance from New Castle northward and westward unto the beginning of the fortieth degree of northern latitude and then by a straight line westward." His Province would thus have embraced the greater part of Maryland, including the city of Baltimore.

In the controversy that ensued Lord Baltimore had the advantage of priority, Penn that of possession and power. In justice to the claims of the latter, however, it should be stated that the map used in making both grants was one published in 1614 by Captain John Smith, in which the location of the fortieth parallel is nearly identical with that of Mason and Dixon's Line.

At an early period in the controversy the Maryland Proprietaries were obliged to concede the claims of the Penns east of the Susquehanna, but they still hoped that west of that river the northern limit of their charter would be recognized. Accordingly, under Governor Ogle's administration strenuous efforts were made to colonize the present territory of York County, Pa., in the Maryland interest and to maintain jurisdiction there by force of arms. A border war ensued, reference of which is especially pertinent here, as two of the most active partisans in the Maryland interest, Cresap and Charlton, subsequently became residents of Leitersburg District. These troubles were terminated in 1738 by a royal order establishing a temporary line, fifteen and one-fourth miles south of Philadelphia east of the Susquehanna; west of the river, fourteen and three-fourth miles south of that city. The latter part of the line was run by Lawrence Growden and Richard Peters, commissioners, and Benjamin Eastburn, surveyor. They began at the Susquehanna on the 8th of May, 1739, and proceeded westward "to the top of the most western hill of a range of hills called the Kittochtinny hills [North mountain], distant from the place of beginning about eighty-eight statute miles."* On the 28th of the same month the survey was reported as completed. The line thus run is known as the Temporary Line. Its course was marked at frequent intervals by blazed trees. In the longitude of Leitersburg District the Temporary Line was about 225 perches north of Mason and Dixon's,† and the intervening territory in Pennsylvania was all secured under Maryland tenure.

It was doubtless expected that a permanent survey would soon supersede the Temporary Line of 1739; but it was not until 1760 that the Penns and Lord Baltimore entered into an agreement by which the controversy was finally terminated. In 1763 Charles Mason and Jeremiah Dixon, two eminent mathematicians and surveyors, were employed to run the lines agreeably to the terms of this agreement. The lines that constitute the present boundaries of the State of Delaware first engaged their attention. In the survey of the line that bears their name they reached the Susquehanna on the 17th of June, 1765, and crossed South mountain about the 1st of September. The following entries occur in their journal during the survey across the Cumberland valley:

September 4. At 93 m. 63 ch. crossed the first rivulet running into Antietam. At 94 m. 62 ch. crossed a second rivulet running into Antietam. This rivulet is at the foot of the South mountain on the west side.

---

* Pennsylvania Archives, Vol. I, p. 613.

† In the office of the county surveyor of Washington County there is a connected draught of Fabian's Marsh, Poor Robin's Almanac, and other tracts, on which the course of the Temporary Line is indicated about twenty-five perches north of the northern point of Fabian's Marsh, which is also the northern point of a tract of land deeded to Joseph M. Bell by the heirs of David Jacobs in 1881. This point is about two hundred perches north of Mason and Dixon's Line between the first and second mile stones west of the Antietam.

EARLY LAND TENURE AND SETTLEMENT. 47

5. Brought the sector to this side of the mountain.
6. Set up the sector in our direction at the distance of 94 m. 63 ch. 10 l. from the post* marked west in Mr. Bryan's field, and made the following observations.

The journal from September 7th to 18th consists entirely of astronomical observations and computations based thereon for the purpose of determining the true parallel.

19. Packing up the instruments, etc.
20. Began to run the line in the direction found per stars on the 9th inst., corrected so as to be in the parallel at 20′ west (supposing us to change at every 10′ as usual).
21. Continued the line. At 95 m. 38 ch. crossed a brook[1] running into Antietam. At 96 m. 3 ch. Mr. Stophel Shockey's house 7 ch. north.
23. Continued the line and crossed Antietam creek at 99 m. 35 ch.
24. Continued the line. At 101 m. 71 ch. Mr. Samuel Irwin's spring[2] house 2 ch. north. At 102 m. 34 ch. Mr. Michael Walker's house 4 ch. north. At 102 m. 67 ch. a rivulet[3] running into Antietam. At 102 m. 70 ch. Mr. William Douglass's house[4] 4 ch. north.
25. Continued the line. At 103 m. 69 ch. crossed a road[5] leading to Swaddinger's Ferry on Potomac.
26. Continued the line. At 105 m. 78 ch. 67 l. changed our direction as usual. At 106 m. 4 ch. Mr. Ludwig Cameron's house 4 ch. north.
27. Continued the line.
28. At 108 m. 5 ch. crossed the road[6] leading from Carlisle to Williams's, now Watkin's Ferry, on Potomac.
30. Continued the line. At 108 m. 65 ch. Mr. Thomas Meek's house 2 ch. south. At 109 m. 14 ch. crossed Conococheague creek.
October 1. Continued the line.
2. Continued the line. At 112 m. 20 ch. crossed a road leading from the Temporary Line to Frederick Town.
3. Continued the line. At 114 m. Mr. Philip Davis's house one mile and a half north by estimation.

---

* The northeastern corner of Maryland, described as "situated in Mill Creek Hundred in the County of New Castle on a plantation belonging to Mr. Alexander Bryan."

[1] Near Midvale station on the Western Maryland railroad.

[2] This spring is on the farm of John H. Miller near the intersection of the line with the Leitersburg and Greencastle road.

[3] Marsh Run.

[4] Near the present residence of Isaac Hykes.

[5] This is probably the road laid out in 1749 under direction of the Frederick County court by Thomas Cresap and Thomas Prather from the Potomac river to the Pennsylvania line "through Salisbury plains."

[6] The present Williamsport and Greencastle road.

4. Continued the line. At 115 m. 42 ch. crossed a small rivulet at the foot of the North mountain.

A series of astronomical observations was begun on the 7th of October, upon the conclusion of which the party returned to the Susquehanna. The journal reads as follows:

> Packed up our instruments and left them (not in the least damaged to our knowledge) at Captain Shelby's.*
> Repaired with Captain Shelby to the summit of the mountain in the direction of our line; but the air was so hazy, prevented our seeing the course of the river.
> 27. Captain Shelby again went with us to the summit of the mountain (when the air was very clear) and showed us the northernmost bend of the river Potomac at the Tonoloways, from which we judge the line will pass about two miles to the north of the said river. From hence we could see the Allegheny mountains for many miles and judge it by appearance to be about fifty miles distance in the direction of the line.
> 28. Set off on our return to the river Susquehanna to mark the offsets from our visto to the true parallel. Set off the offsets to the 109th mile post.
> 29. Set off the offsets to the 96th mile post.
> 30. Set off the offsets to the 87th mile post.

They reached the Susquehanna on the 6th of November and on the 8th "discharged all hands." The westward survey was resumed on the 1st of April, 1766. Sideling Hill creek, the western boundary of Washington County, was crossed on the 29th of April, and the party reached the foot of Savage mountain early in June. The following entry occurs under date of June 18th:

> Set up a post (18 inches square, 3 feet in the ground and 5 out) at the distance of 3.66 chains north of the sector, marked M on the south side, P on the north side, and W on the west, and began to cut a visto in the true parallel or line between Maryland and Pennsylvania by running it through points we have laid off from the line we have made at every ten chains.

They reached the 118th mile post, on the North mountain, July 19th; the 107th, near Mason-Dixon station on the Cumberland Valley railroad, on the 26th; the 96th, near Ringgold, Md., on the 2d of August; and the 85th, east of the South mountain, on the 9th. On the 25th of September this work was completed to "the intersection of the meridian from the tangent point with

---
* Evan Shelby, father of Isaac Shelby, the first Governor of Kentucky.

EARLY LAND TENURE AND SETTLEMENT.

the parallel"—the northeastern corner of the Province of Maryland. Regarding this visto the following entry occurs in the journal under date of September 25th:

> From any eminence in the line where fifteen or twenty miles of the visto can be seen (of which there are many) the said line or visto very apparently shows itself to form a true parallel of northern latitude. The line is measured horizontal; the hills and mountains, with a 16½ foot level.
> Besides the mile posts we have set posts in the true line (marked W on the west side) all along the line opposite the stationary points where the sector and transit instruments stood. The said posts stand in the middle of the visto, which in general is about eight yards wide.

It thus appears that Mason and Dixon crossed the Cumberland valley three times in making their survey. The line run from east to west in September and October, 1765, was not the true line, but its variation from the true line at intervals of ten chains was determined by astronomical observation and computation. The true line was marked from west to east in October, 1765, at eight points in every mile, determined by measurement from the line first run. The true line through the points thus determined and marked was finally run in July and August, 1766, when the visto thereon was also cut out, and here again the surveyors proceeded from west to east. But the work was not yet completed. In 1768 stones were planted at the end of every fifth mile engraved with the arms of the Penns on the north side and those of the Calverts on the south side; the intermediate miles were marked with stones engraved with the letter P on the north side and M on the south. These stones were imported from England.

A five-mile stone stands near the eastern line of Leitersburg District, between the farm of William H. Hoffman in Maryland and that of John Bonebrake in Pennsylvania, and another formerly stood at the terminus of the Marsh turnpike, where it formed the northwestern corner of the District. Of the four intermediate mile stones along the District line three still stand, located as follows: On the farm of Mrs. C. B. Deitrich, east of Antietam creek; west of that stream, between the lands of Augustus Shiffler in Maryland and David B. Shoemaker in Pennsylvania, and between the lands of Franklin M. Strite in Maryland

and those of Henry Barkdoll in Pennsylvania; the fourth formerly stood on the farm of John H. Miller, three perches west of the Leitersburg and Greencastle road.

The surveyors were accompanied by a full complement of assistants, including laborers, axemen, wagoners, etc. In September, 1767, far to the westward of Fort Cumberland, twenty-six of their assistants deserted through fear of the Indians and only fifteen axemen remained, from which it is evident that the party numbered about fifty persons. From July 19 to August 9, 1766, they cut out the visto at the rate of eleven miles per week, an average of nearly two miles per day, as it is evident from the journal that no labor was performed on Sunday. This visto consituated the first road to Jacobs church and doubtless determined the selection of its site.

CHAPTER II.

Social and Material Development.

Language, Dress, Etc.—Slavery—Erection and Boundaries of Leitersburg District—Politics—"In War Times"—Agricultural Development—Postal Facilities—Public Roads—Bridges—Turnpikes—Mills—Rock Forge—Distilleries—Tanneries, Textile Manufactures, Etc.

With respect to nationality the pioneers of Leitersburg District were almost exclusively German. Cresap, Charlton, Perry, and Sprigg were English, and Gabby was Scotch, but their names are almost forgotten. The German element was represented by such names as Lambert, Miller, Shiess, Burkhart, Hartle, Fogler, Leiter, Good, Ritter, Reiff, Bell, Lantz, Schriver, Solmes, Snell, Mentzer, Garver, Stotler, Wolfinger, Ziegler, Strite—an overwhelming majority; and many of these families are still represented, because the Germans, as a class, came to stay.

Industry and thrift, the tendency to acquire real estate and to retain it when acquired, are characteristics of the Teuton, and while there is abundant reason to believe that the early German settlers were generally poor, they were not long in securing homes and providing for their families the necessities and comforts of life. The second generation started in life with larger capital and better advantages than the first; its numbers were reduced by emigration, but reenforced again from the older German communities of York and Lancaster Counties in Pennsylvania, and thus the District became more thoroughly German than before. The poll and tax books still show an almost uninterrupted succession of German names, Anglicized in orthography and pronunciation but German nevertheless. The four religious denominations represented in the District—Lutheran, Reformed, Mennonite, and German Baptist—are all of German origin. For several generations German was the language of social and business intercourse with a large majority of the population; it was the language of public worship at Jacobs church until 1840, and at Miller's church at a still later date. To-day it is a dead language, and in this respect the pioneers have failed to transmit to their posterity that to which they most tenaciously adhered. But English was the language of the county courts, of the local schoolmaster, and of the country at large, and under such a combination of influences the transition to its use, though gradual, was inevitable.

The change in language was accompanied by others equally noticeable. "The dress of the early settlers," says Kercheval in his History of the Valley of Virginia, "was of the plainest material, generally of their own manufacture. The men's coats were generally made with broad backs and straight short skirts, with pockets on the outside having large flaps. The waist-coats had skirts nearly halfway down to the knees and very broad pocket-flaps. The breeches were so short as barely to reach the knee, with a band surrounding the knee, fastened with either brass or silver buckles. The stocking was drawn up under the knee band and tied with a garter (generally red or blue) below the knee, so as to be seen. Shoes were of coarse leather, with straps to the quarters and fastened with either brass or silver buckles. The hat was either of wool or felt, with a round crown not exceeding three or four inches in height with a broad brim. The dress for the neck was usually a narrow collar to the shirt, with a white linen stock drawn together at the ends on the back of the neck with a broad metal buckle. The more wealthy and fashionable were sometimes seen with their stock, knee, and shoe buckles set in gold or silver with precious stones. * * * The female dress was generally the short gown and petticoat made of the plainest materials. The German women mostly wore tight calico caps on their heads. * * * In hay and harvest time they joined the men in the labors of the meadow and grain fields. * * * Many females were most expert mowers and reapers. It was no uncommon thing to see the female part of the family at the hoe or plow." To this it might be added that men, women, and children alike discarded shoes in warm weather, on the score of comfort as well as economy. While respect for the church was almost universal, it was not considered necessary to wear a coat in warm weather, when the men usually appeared in their shirt sleeves. There are those still living who remember when this was characteristic of the congregations at Beard's and Jacobs.

The first farm improvements usually consisted of a log house and barn, built near a spring or running water if the land offered such advantages. The floor of the primitive cabin was made of split puncheons and the roof of clapboards weighted with poles. Hewn logs, a shingled or thatched roof, and plank floors indicated an improvement in the circumstances of the owner. A few houses of more pretentious appearance were also built at an early date. The stone house on the farm of Daniel N. Scheller, near the Ziegler mill and several rods beyond the District line, was built by Samuel Downing in 1750, and is undoubtedly one of the oldest specimens of colonial architecture in Washington County. The oldest part of the farm house on the farm of Hiram D. Middlekauff near Leitersburg was built by John Gabby prior to 1779. Among the oldest stone houses within the limits of the District is that on the farm of George F. Ziegler near Leitersburg, built by George Lantz, who died in 1802. In 1803 Henry B. Hockman built the stone house near Bowman's mill owned by the heirs of Henry G. Clopper. Frederick Bell built the stone house on the farm of Daniel S. Wolfinger near Rock Forge in 1812. In 1823 Andrew Bell built the stone house on the farm of Upton Clopper. The stone house on the farm of Harvey J. Hartle, near Leitersburg, and that on the farm of Isaac Shank, near the Marsh mills, are also among the oldest representatives of the stone age in rural architecture in Leitersburg District. The oldest brick house is undoubtedly that on the Cressler farm, built by General Sprigg in the last century.

Stone was also used so far as possible in the construction of barns. Frederick Bell built the stone barn on the farm of Daniel S. Wolfinger in 1806; John Barr, that on the farm of Harvey J. Hartle, in 1809; Michael Wolfinger, that on the farm owned by the heirs of the late Joseph Strite, in 1815; Joseph Miller, that on the farm of Samuel Hykes, in 1819; John Mentzer, that on the farm of E. Keller Mentzer, in 1826. A number of others were also built, principally at a later date. It seems somewhat surprising that the enormous stone gables of these structures should have been reared at a time when timber was plenty and possessed but little commercial value.

A hundred years ago the aristocracy of Washington County lived in the country, and of this class the most distinguished representative in Leitersburg District was General Thomas Sprigg. His estate was Sprigg's Paradise, a tract of seventeen hundred acres. Here he erected a spacious mansion, some description of which may not be inappropriate. The main hall is sixty-two feet long and twelve feet wide, and at each end there was originally a winding stairway. The drawing room, dining room, etc. connected with this hall. The ceilings are fourteen feet high on the first floor and thirteen on the second. The house is constructed throughout in a most substantial manner and finished with a degree of care, taste, and expense rarely found in Washington County country residences at the present day. The culinary department and the servants' quarters occupied a separate wing. East of the mansion was the garden, arranged in a series of terraces. The estate was cultivated by slaves, whose quarters, a long, low stone building near the turnpike, were removed several years ago. The establishment also included a race track, west of the turnpike, one mile in length and sixty feet wide, with woods on either side.

This old mansion was often the scene of protracted festivities, in which horse-racing, fox-hunting, cock-baiting, dancing, and other fashionable amusements contributed to the diversion of the guests. The General and his son, who succeeded him, dispensed a lavish hospitality. Their immediate circle included the families of Major Ignatius Taylor, Thomas Belt, and Thomas Hall, all of whom resided in Leitersburg District, and Charles Carroll of Bellevue, an estate of a thousand acres near Hagerstown. The *elite* of Washington County were entertained here, and visits were also exchanged with families of wealth and prominence in southern Maryland. But Sprigg's Paradise has shared the same fate as Fountain Rock, Montpelier, and every other large landed estate in the county. The old mansion still stands, a reminder of social and material conditions that are forever past, but only a fraction of the estate is connected with it in ownership, and the family name in which the title was vested for three generations is now unfamiliar or forgotten.

SLAVERY IN THE DISTRICT.

There is evidence that slavery existed upon the present territory of Leitersburg District at an early period in its history.

Robert Downing, who died in 1755, bequeathed to his son Robert "one negro man named Will and one negro woman named Rachel;" and to his son Samuel "one negro boy named Dick and one negro girl named Kate."

The following are transcripts of original papers relating to slavery in the District at a later date:

Received, January 21, 1804, of Jacob Miller the sum of £18 for hire of negro Jem, the property of Letty Hall, for one year ending 20th January, 1804.   I. TAYLOR.

Received, January 20, 1806, of Mr. Jacob Miller $80.00 on account of Miss Letty Hall for the hire of two negros, Jem and Bob, for one year ending this day.   THOMAS BELT.

To all whom it may concern: Be it known that I, Jacob Miller, of Washington County in the State of Maryland, for divers good causes and considerations me thereunto moving as also in further consideration of one dollar current money to me in hand paid, have released from slavery, liberated, manumitted, and set free from and after the 1st day of January in the year of our Lord 1825 * * * my negro man named John Norrison, who will at the date aforesaid be of the age of thirty years and if in health be able to work and gain a sufficient livelihood and maintenance, and him the said negro man named John Norrison I do declare to be from and after the 1st day of January, 1825, aforesaid free, manumitted, and discharged from all manner of servitude or service to me, my executors, or administrators forever. In testimony whereof I have hereunto set my hand and affixed my seal this 26th of July in the year of our Lord 1820.
    JACOB MILLER.

Know all men by these presents that I, Jacob Kessinger of Washington County and State of Maryland for the consideration of the sum of $145.00 current money to me in hand paid by John Mentzer, Jr., of the county and State aforesaid, the receipt whereof I do hereby acknowledge, have granted, bargained, sold, and delivered * * * unto the said John Mentzer, Jr., my negro slave Betty, which said slave Betty I will warrant and defend to the said John Mentzer, Jr., his executors, administrators, and assigns * * * against every other person or persons whomsoever. In witness whereof I have hereunto set my name and affixed my seal this 13th day of March, 1820.   JACOB KESSINGER.

It is my will that my colored people, viz., Hannah Reed, Benjamin Buchanan, and Joseph Smith, be free immediately after my death, and that my executors pay to each of them * * * the sum of $150 apiece.—*Will of William Gabby.*

In 1815 Christian Lantz manumitted his slave Charles Bryson, aged thirty-eight years, at the consideration of $600.00. In 1827 William Gabby manumitted his "negro woman named Jemima, being at the age of thirty-five years, and able to work and gain a sufficient livelihood and maintenance," at the consideration of one dollar. Among other slave-owners in the District were the Spriggs, Thomas Belt, George I. Harry, Jacob Schnebley, Joseph Gabby, George Shiess, and F. C. B. Wilms. It is probable that the number of slaves kept on the Sprigg estate was equal to those of all other owners in the District combined. At her death in 1851 Mrs. Maria E. Reynolds (*nee* Sprigg) owned twelve slaves, of whom the youngest was twelve years of age and the oldest eighty. By the terms of her will they all received manumission and substantial legacies. Chatham Jones, who thus secured his freedom after eighty years of servitude, lived to the age of more than a hundred and is still remembered by old residents of the Marsh neighborhood, to whom he used to relate that he was brought to Paradise by General Thomas Sprigg and employed as a young man in the building of the old Marsh mill and other improvements on the Paradise estate.

Slavery was never a flourishing institution in Leitersburg District, because there were few estates of sufficient size to render slave labor profitable. Emancipations were frequently made, as shown in the preceding pages, and it is doubtful whether a single slave remained in the District to be liberated by the constitution of 1864.

Erection and Boundaries of Leitersburg District.

Antietam and Salisbury Hundreds, erected by the Frederick County court in 1749, with Antietam creek as a mutual boundary, embraced the present territory of Leitersburg District. Both were subsequently divided, the former in 1758 and the latter at a later date, after which the District was embraced in Upper Antietam and Upper Salisbury until 1824, when hundreds were no longer recognized as political subdivisions in Washington County.

For many years after the organization of the county elections were held at Hagerstown. In 1800 five election districts were established, of which No. 3 included the northeastern part of the county. This extensive district was bounded on the west by Conococheague creek and the Williamsport and Greencastle road,

Some explanation of the original boundaries of the District may not be inappropriate. "The Greencastle and Hagerstown road" is now known as the Hagerstown and Middleburg turnpike; "Frederick Ziegler's mill" is situated on Marsh run and is now owned by his son, David Ziegler; "the Hagerstown and Waynesboro road" is the Marsh turnpike and the Nicholson's Gap road is the Hagerstown and Leitersburg turnpike; "Bachtel's school house" was situated near Fiddlersburg on the farm of Martin Bachtel, now owned by the Loose estate; "John Wolfersberger's ford on the Antietam creek" is the ford at Trovinger's mill.

The boundary thus established embraced an area probably twice as great as that of the District at the present time. Unfortunately, however, the work of the boundary commission was not entirely satisfactory, and within a few years after the erection of the District its territory was materially reduced. This was effected by an act of the Legislature passed on the 10th of March, 1841, by which the line between District No. 3 and District No. 9 was established agreeably to the following description:

Beginning at the Pennsylvania line where the Waynesboro road crosses the same, and running with said road to the Paradise school house, and from thence with the public road to Frederick Ziegler's mill, and from thence with a straight line to the end of Peter Spessard's lane on the road leading from the Forge mill to Hagerstown, and thence with said road to the fording at the Forge mill, where it intersects the original location of said Ninth Election District.

This established the present western and southwestern boundaries of the District. The present eastern boundary was established by the erection of Ringgold District, June 12, 1860; this line is described as "Beginning on the line dividing the States of Maryland and Pennsylvania at a point about two hundred yards west from Frick's foundry and in the center of a public road"—a point it might be difficult to identify, as both foundry and road have gone out of existence. The present southern boundary from the Old Forge road to a point beyond Antietam creek was established in 1872 by the erection of Chewsville District. The Old Forge road continued to be the southeastern boundary of the District until September 5, 1882, when the present line between Districts No. 7 and No. 9 (Cavetown and Leitersburg) as surveyed by S. S. Downin was confirmed by the county commissioners.

SOCIAL AND MATERIAL DEVELOPMENT. 57

on the north by the State line, and on the east by the South mountain, with Orr's Gap as its southern limit; it included Hagerstown, and there elections were held at the court house. In 1822 the territory of District No. 3 was materially reduced by the erection of District No. 7 (Cavetown), a measure of much importance to the region subsequently embraced in District No. 9 (Leitersburg). The Greencastle road from the State line to Antietam creek and that stream for a distance of some miles to the south were constituted the line of division between Nos. 3 and 7. West of the Greencastle road and Antietam creek the citizens continued to vote at Hagerstown, as they had done since 1776; east of that line the polling place was at Cavetown. This arrangement continued until 1838, when Leitersburg District was erected. The original act of the Legislature establishing the District was passed on the 6th of March, 1837. It provided for the erection of an additional election district in Washington County to be composed of parts of the Seventh and Third, and Lewis Ziegler, John Byer, and Jacob Bell were appointed commissioners to establish the boundaries. As this involved an amendment to the constitution, concurrent legislation at the ensuing session was necessary before it became operative. A confirmatory act was duly passed on the 14th of March, 1838, and thus, so far as legislative action was concerned, Leitersburg District became a separate and distinct subdivision of the county and State. The boundary commission met at the court house in Hagerstown on the 29th of March, 1838, and after three days' deliberation established the following boundary for the Ninth Election District:

Beginning at the red post in the town of Middleburg on the Pennsylvania line, thence with the Greencastle and Hagerstown road to where the road from Frederick Ziegler's mill intersects said road, thence with said Ziegler's road to Paradise school house, thence with the Hagerstown and Waynesboro road to the finger-board where the Nicholson's Gap road intersects said road, thence with a straight line to Bachtel's school house, thence with a straight line to John Wolfersberger's ford on the Antietam creek, thence with said creek to the Forge mill, thence to Beard's church, thence with the road to Welty's church and school house, thence with said road to the Pennsylvania line, thence with said line to the place of beginning.

DISTRICT POLITICS.

On the 20th of March, 1838, the Legislature passed an act directing the commissioners of Washington County to appoint a place for holding elections in Leitersburg District and appoint judges for the same. The first election was accordingly held on the first Wednesday in October, 1838, when Samuel Lyday was elected to represent the new District in the board of county commissioners.

The constitution of Maryland confers upon local election districts a very limited measure of political autonomy. There was a time when each district elected a county commissioner and a local constable; when the board of county commissioners appointed a district supervisor of roads, with jurisdiction over all the public roads of the district, and a district school commissioner, with similar functions in connnection with its educational work. But at the present time all administrative functions are centralized at the county seat and the district is a geographical rather than a political subdivision. No local offices are elective. Justices of the peace and registers of voters are appointed by the Governor; election officers, by the county board; constables and supervisors of roads, by the county commissioners; school trustees, by the county school board. Consequently, the larger issues of the county, State, and nation engross the attention in district politics; there is no contest over local officers and measures.

This does not imply an apathetic or indifferent attitude toward partisan politics; on the contrary, the great national political parties have always had stanch and stalwart supporters in Leitersburg District. A presidential campaign usually develops all the latent political enthusiasm and party loyalty, and that of 1840, the first after the organization of the District, is generally regarded as one of the most exciting the country has ever known. The Democratic primary, as reported in the Hagerstown *Mail*, was held on the 13th of June at the house of James Weaver. Joseph Trovinger was chairman, Benjamin Hartman vice-chairman, and John P. Stephey secretary. A committee of three, composed of Joseph Leiter, William E. Doyle, and William N. Rolls, was appointed by the chairman to select delegates to the county convention and reported the names of Joseph Trovinger, David T. Wilson, William E. Doyle, Joseph Leiter, William N.

Rolls, John P. Stephey, Samuel Etnyer, David Bell, Henry Brumbaugh, Hugh Logan, Ignatius Brown, and Abner Hays. Jacob E. Bell was nominated for county commissioner. The county convention was held on the 20th of June, when Samuel Lyday, of Leitersburg District, was one of the nominees for the House of Delegates.

The Whig primary meeting was advertised to be held "in District No. 9 at the Log Cabin in Leitersburg," but no account of its proceedings was published in the *Torch Light*. Lewis Tritle was nominated for county commissioner, but before the election he was superseded by George Poe. Joseph Gabby of Leitersburg District presided over the county convention, and among his colleagues as delegates were Charles A. Fletcher and David Brumbaugh. Lewis Ziegler was one of the nominees for House of Delegates. In the Whig convention for the nomination of a presidential elector for the Sixth Congressional district, No. 9 was represented by Joseph Gabby, Dr. T. B. Duckett, and Charles A. Fletcher. The District member of the county central committee was D. G. Martin.

As the campaign advanced the enthusiasm on both sides became intense. Immense public meetings attended by thousands of people were held at Hagerstown by both parties, to each of which Leitersburg District sent a numerous equestrian delegation. Nor was the proper education of local public sentiment neglected; both parties held large and enthusiastic meetings at Leitersburg, when suffrages were sought by fervid oratory and persuasive eloquence, reenforced on the part of the Whigs by copious supplies of hard cider.

The judges of election were William Webb, Joseph Trovinger, and Peter Bell. The number of votes received by the respective candidates was as follows: Bell, 169; Poe, 177; Lyday, 194; Ziegler, 193; Van Buren, 185; Harrison, 177. The "Log Cabin and Hard Cider" campaign having resulted in the national triumph of the Whigs, Frederick Ziegler of Leitersburg District sent a barrel of cider to the White House shortly after the inauguration of President Harrison. His wagoner delivered it with the six-horse team—a very unusual proceeding, notwithstanding which it was accepted by the President and duly acknowledged as a congratulatory testimonial from a loyal member of his party.

SOCIAL AND MATERIAL DEVELOPMENT.

The vote for President, so far as ascertainable, since the erection of the District has been as follows:

1840.—Martin Van Buren, Democrat, 185; William Henry Harrison, Whig, 177.
1844.—James K. Polk, Democrat, 168; Henry Clay, Whig, 180.
1848.—Lewis Cass, Democrat, 152; Zachary Taylor, Whig, 190.
1852.—Franklin Pierce, Democrat, 171; Winfield Scott, Whig, 187.
1868.—Horatio Seymour, Democrat, 121; Ulysses S. Grant, Republican, 183.
1872.—Ulysses S. Grant, Republican, 174; Horace Greeley, Liberal Republican, 111.
1876.—Samuel J. Tilden, Democrat, 131; Rutherford B. Hayes, Republican, 180.
1880.—Winfield S. Hancock, Democrat, 127; James A. Garfield, Republican, 185.
1884.—Grover Cleveland, Democrat, 116; James G. Blaine, Republican, 179; John P. St. John, Prohibitionist, 1.
1888.—Grover Cleveland, Democrat, 124; Benjamin Harrison, Republican, 169; Clinton B. Fisk, Prohibitionist, 6.
1892.—Grover Cleveland, Democrat, 132; Benjamin Harrison, Republican, 162; John Bidwell, Prohibitionist, 6.
1896.—William J. Bryan, Democrat, 114; William McKinley, Republican, 163; Joshua Levering, Prohibitionist, 9; John R. Palmer, Independent Democrat, 2.

The official representation of the District has been as follows:

Member of Congress.—1792-96, Thomas Sprigg.

Member of State Convention to Ratify the Constitution of the United States.—1788, Thomas Sprigg.

Members of Constitutional Conventions.—1864, James P. Mayhugh; 1867, George W. Pole.

Presidential Elector.—1821, William Gabby.

Members of House of Delegates.—1784, Thomas Hart; 1787-88, Ignatius Taylor; 1788, Thomas Sprigg; 1807-8, William Gabby; 1810-11, Thomas B. Hall; 1812, William O. Sprigg; 1813-14, William Gabby; 1819-23, Joseph Gabby; 1826, Thomas B. Hall; 1838-39, Frederick Byer; 1840, Lewis Ziegler; 1841, Samuel Lyday; 1844, Charles A. Fletcher; 1846, William E. Doyle, Joseph Leiter; 1847, George L. Ziegler; 1863-64, Frederick K. Ziegler.

Register of Wills.—Thomas Sprigg, 1776-80; Thomas Belt, 1780-1806; William Logan, 1857-67.

Justices of the Levy Court.—1806-9, Thomas Sprigg; 1820, William Gabby; 1823-29, Joseph Gabby.

County Commissioners.—1838, Samuel Lyday; 1840, George Poe; 1844, William E. Doyle; 1857, Daniel Mentzer; 1865, Frederick Bell; 1871, Samuel Strite.

Judges of the Orphans' Court.—1806-7, Ignatius Taylor; 1812, Thomas B. Hall; 1821-24, William Gabby; 1875-79, Samuel Strite.

Collectors of County Taxes.—1847, William E. Doyle; 1849, William Logan; 1864-65, Samuel F. Ziegler; 1876-77, William M. Lantz.

Sheriffs.—1853-55, William Logan; 1879-81, Frederick K. Ziegler.

School Commissioners.—1864, James P. Mayhugh; 1868, Edward Smith; 1871, James D. Slaughenhaupt; 1881-91, Samuel Strite.

Justices of the Peace.—Thomas Sprigg, William Webb, William Gabby, Christopher Burkhart, Joseph Gabby, Thomas B. Hall, William Kreps, George H. Lambert, Hugh Logan, Benjamin Hartman, Samuel Lyday, Francis C. Shiess, James P. Mayhugh, James A. Hays, Peter Middlekauff, John Lambert, Lewis J. Ground, Frank D. Bell.

POPULATION AND WEALTH.

In 1860 the population of the District was 1,962; in 1870, 1,673; in 1880, 1,546; in 1890, 1,368.

The value of the different species of property in the District in 1897, as shown by the records of the county commissioners, was as follows: Real estate, $569,636; private securities, $45,671; bonds, etc., $2,648; stock in trade, $7,607; personal property, $78,201; exemptions, $14,803.

"IN WAR TIMES."

England and Spain were at war in 1740, and although Western Maryland was far from the scene of conflict the war brought financial disaster to one of the pioneers of Leitersburg District. Colonel Thomas Cresap had collected at his trading post at Longmeadows a quantity of valuable furs, and the ship by which they were consigned to England was captured by the enemy, reducing

SOCIAL AND MATERIAL DEVELOPMENT. 63

him to bankruptcy and necessitating his departure from Longmeadows in the following year.

In the French and Indian War (1755-63) the enemy made frequent incursions into the Cumberland valley, but if any Indian atrocities were committed in Leitersburg District no record of the fact has been preserved. There is a tradition that Antietam church near Trovinger's mill was converted into a blockhouse and was a place of rendezvous for the surrounding country in time of threatened danger. In his will, dated February 8, 1764, Jacob Leiter of Leitersburg District inserted this clause: "I ordain that if any of my estate shall be destroyed or carried away by the enemy that my executors shall not be subject to loss thereby." It was Colonel Henry Bouquet, the owner of the Longmeadows estate in Leitersburg District, who defeated the Indians at the decisive battle of Bushy Run, August 5-6, 1763, and led a victorious expedition against the Ohio tribes in the following year.

The various schemes of colonial taxation devised by the British government at the close of the French and Indian war elicited energetic protests from the people of Western Maryland, and when the Continental Congress declared against the importation of taxable articles the people of Frederick County assembled at the county seat, November 18, 1774, and appointed a general committee to carry into effect the resolves of Congress; among the members of this committee were Joseph Perry and Christopher Burkhart, of Leitersburg District, of whom the former was also a member of the county committee of correspondence. At a meeting at Frederick on the 24th of January, 1775, they were again appointed members of the county committee "to carry the resolves of the American Congress and of the Provincial Convention into execution." Local committees were also appointed for every hundred in the county to solicit subscriptions for the purchase of arms and ammunition. Leitersburg District was then included in Upper Antietam and Salisbury Hundreds; for the former the committee consisted of Jonathan Hager, Dr. Henry Schnebley, and Jacob Zeller; for the latter, of Jacob Funk, Conrad Hogmire, Joseph Perry, and John Ingram. They were instructed "to apply personally or by deputy to every freeman in their respective districts and to solicit a generous contribution." In the Committee of Observation for Washington County Leitersburg District was represented by Christian Lantz and Christopher

Burkhart. There can be no doubt that the District contributed a fair quota of men to the Continental army, but unfortunately no record of their names or services is now accessible.*

In the War of 1812 the militia of Washington County was called out *en masse*, August 25, 1814, by General Samuel Ringgold and mobilized at Boonsboro on the following day. The company from Leitersburg District was commanded by Captain John Byer and embraced practically all the citizens of the District capable of bearing arms. A British army had routed the forces opposed to it as Bladensburg, Md., and burned the national Capitol at Washington; General Ringgold called out his brigade with the conviction that its services would be necessary in contesting the further advance of the enemy. But the Secretary of War regarded the forces already at his disposal as sufficient for the emergency and on the 28th, the brigade having been disbanded, Captain Byer and his company returned to their homes. The District was also represented at the battle of Baltimore and in the Canada campaign of the preceding year.

For some years the State maintained a militia organization and the citizens in every locality were required by law to muster for practice in military drill and discipline. Thomas Sprigg, of Leitersburg District, was commissioned as lieutenant colonel for Washington County in 1794 and subsequently rose to the rank of brigadier general. Regimental musters were held for some years on his estate, and company musters at Captain Byer's mill, near Leitersburg, subsequently owned by Fowler & Ziegler, at Schmutz's mill, now the property of David Ziegler, and on the farm of David Hoover, near Beard's church. Something of the spirit of the old militia days is reflected in the following notices, originally published in contemporary newspapers:

---

* On the 30th of December, 1776, the County Committee ordered the militia to march to the assistance of General Washington and appointed a number of persons to "collect all the people who may be left after the militia have marched and form themselves into companies and choose their own officers for the purpose of relieving the distress of the inhabitants." Among the persons so appointed were Christopher Burkhart, Jacob Ritter, Peter Shiess, Wendell Sights, George Lambert, Joseph Perry, and John Gabby of Leitersburg District.

The following entry occurs in the minutes of the County Committee, January 10, 1777: "WHEREAS, Complaint has been made to this Committee that no horses have yet been procured in order to draw the cannon for the use of Colonel Stull's battalion : *Ordered*, That Jacob Good furnish one team for that purpose ; in case the said Good can not furnish four horses his own property, that he apply to some neighbor to assist him therein, who is hereby required to be assistive." Good was a resident of Leitersburg District.

SOCIAL AND MATERIAL DEVELOPMENT.

The companies commanded by Captains Wellar, Lantz, Rench, and Allen are desired to meet at General Sprigg's quarter on Saturday, the 29th inst., to exercise in battalion agreeably to law.

CHARLES CARROLL, *Major.*

Elizabeth-Town, August 18, 1795.

Hagerstown, September 19, 1799.

ORDERED, That the Eighth Regiment of the Second Brigade of militia be paraded on Saturday, the 19th of October next, the Tenth Regiment on the 22d, and the Twenty-fourth Regiment on the 26th day of the same month, each at 9 o'clock in the morning.

T. SPRIGG,
Brig. Gen., Second Brigade.

Attention! You are hereby ordered to parade in company at Mr. Abraham Schmutz's mill on the second Saturday in May next and at Captain Byer's mill on the last Saturday in August next at 2 o'clock p. m. A court martial to try the absentees of both the above parades will sit at Captain Byer's on the last Saturday in September next at 2 o'clock p. m.

JOSEPH TROVINGER, *Captain.*

March 26, 1825.

The court martial was accordingly held and the following is a transcript of its proceedings:

At a court martial held at Mr. John Byer's in Washington County on Saturday, the 24th day of September, 1825, composed of Lieutenant Archibald Halbert, Sergeant John Daniel, Private D. T. Wilson, the following delinquents were tried for their non-attendance at the company parade on Saturday, the 27th day of August, 1825, belonging to Captain Joseph Trovinger's company, Eighth Regiment, Maryland militia:

John McVey, out of the State at the time, acquitted.			Daniel Jacobs,	Fined	$1 00
			Lewis Ziegler,	"	1 00
Jacob Byer, lame knee, acquitted.			John Strite,	"	1 00
			Samuel Miller of Jos.,	"	1 00
Joseph Emmert,	Fined	$1 00	John Wolfersberger,	"	1 00
Samuel Bachtel,	"	1 00	John Coursey,	"	1 00
Abraham Strite,	"	1 00	William Minor,	"	1 00
Samuel Strite,	"	1 00	Nathan Davis,	"	1 00
Joseph Strite,	"	1 00	Isaac Hammaker,	"	1 00

We do certify that the above statement is a true copy of the proceedings of this court martial.

ARCHIBALD HALBERT, *Lieutenant.*
JOHN DANIEL, *Sergeant.*
D. T. WILSON, *Private.*

Many delinquencies were due to conscientious considerations, as the principles of the Mennonite and other religious bodies do not permit participation in military exercises. Some original papers showing the operation of the law in such cases are still preserved, several of which are herewith given:

Received, April 2, 1800, of Jacob Miller $3.00 for his muster fines due for the year 1799.   J. McPHERSON, *Deputy Sheriff.*

I hereby certify and make known that I have reason to believe and verily do believe from the religious and exemplary deportment of and uniform declaration of Jacob Newcomer that he is conscientiously scrupulous of bearing arms and that I consider him as belonging to the Mennonist society under my direction. Given under my hand this 28th day of May, 1818.
                                         JOHN STOUFFER.

Received, March 24, 1821, of John Newcomer $9.00 in full for militia fines against John, Andrew, and Jacob Newcomer for the year 1820.
                               SAMUEL EICHELBERGER, *Deputy Collector.*

In the Civil War the District became for the first time the scene of military movements on a grand scale. Before the battle of Gettysburg (July 1, 2, 3, 1863) one division of the Confederate army passed through Leitersburg and on Saturday night, July 4th, the Confederate wagon train passed through the village, followed on Monday morning by the army, which marched continuously until 2 o'clock p. m. on Tuesday. The main body, consisting of infantry, cavalry, and artillery, passed over the turnpike, but all the by-roads leading southward were also crowded. General Lee and several of his division commanders were recognized by the citizens as they passed through Leitersburg.

The Confederate invasions of 1862 and 1863 occasioned great alarm in Washington County and many farmers and others from Leitersburg District joined in the general "skedaddle." Horses, wagons, and other movable property were hurried over the mountains in the direction of interior Pennsylvania, for which there was abundant reason, as such property was freely appropriated by both armies and especially by the irresponsible parties of stragglers that followed them.

The following is a list of Federal soldiers who enlisted from Leitersburg District:

William Anderson,	Martin Maugans,
Abram Avey,	Jacob A. Metz,

SOCIAL AND MATERIAL DEVELOPMENT.

Samuel Arey,
Philip M. Bell,
John Boner,
John Gagle,
Solomon Gagle,
Benjamin F. Garver,
Daniel Garver,
James A. Hays,
Joshua Hellman,
David V. High,
Jacob Hovis,
Thomas Hughes,
Samuel Kline,
William Kline,
Charles E. H. Koppisch,
George U. Lowman,
Jacob F. Lowman,

—— Miller,
Abram Mowry,
John Mowry,
Polk Mowry,
Solomon Myers,
John W. Nigh,
Samuel T. Nigh,
Gabby Nofford,
Robert Slick,
David Stephey,
William Stephey,
Daniel Tritle,
John Wampler,
Frederick Ziegler,
George Ziegler,
James R. Ziegler.

Perhaps no event of the Civil War excited so much horror in Leitersburg District as the murder of Edward Gladfelter. He reached Leitersburg on the 26th of August, 1864, in charge of some horses belonging to a Federal officer; there he was stopped by four Federal cavalrymen, who took his horses and compelled him to accompany them on foot, and at a point a mile north of the village on the turnpike he was murdered. The perpetrators, Coon, Forney, and Riley, were apprehended near Hagerstown and delivered to the civil authorities. They were tried at March term, 1865, and convicted. In pronouncing sentence Judge French said: "On the road running the boy was seen delivering to you his silver watch. A little farther on you were seen robbing his body. as he stood pale and trembling in your power, of his money, his pocketbook, his comb, etc. You then took him to the next hill and there wilfully and deliberately blew his brains out with a pistol or gun. Edward Gladfelter fell at your horses' feet in the middle of the high road, a murderd man, a lifeless body. Then you left him on the public road to welter in his gore and returned shouting, soon after the pistol shot was heard, through Leitersburg. In all the annals of crime I have never read of so foul, so black, so inhuman a murder."

In the war with Spain the District is represented by Lieutenant Strite, U. S. N., and Keller Lowman, a private in the Douglas Guards. Lieutenant Strite's ship is the *Olympia*, the flag-ship of the Asiatic squadron, which participated in the battle of Manila, May 1, 1898.

POSTAL FACILITIES.

The following is a list of postmasters at Leitersburg, with the dates of their respective appointments: Joshua Grimes, May 9, 1826; Charles A. Fletcher, March 21, 1829; Samuel Etnyer, December 8, 1838; Charles H. Besore, February 17, 1841; David M. Good, June 7, 1843; James P. Mayhugh, September 19, 1845; Jacob Kissell, May 7, 1847; David M. Deitrich, June 9, 1849; Samuel F. Ziegler, January 13, 1851; Benjamin F. Slick, April 26, 1853; Daniel S. Wolfinger, March 19, 1861; James A. Hays, December 18, 1865; Samuel Ziegler, April 22, 1869; John H. Ziegler, January 28, 1871; John W. Nigh, May 27, 1872; Frederick Koppisch, January 6, 1873; Charles E. H. Koppisch, May 6, 1884; David Barnhart, May 19, 1885; Alice Ziegler, May 28, 1889; David Barnhart, March 10, 1894; Jacob M. Stouffer, April, 1898.

Frank Trovinger was appointed postmaster at Startown, May 3, 1894; William R. Trovinger, October 14, 1895; Samuel Hartman, February 6, 1896.

George H. Bowman was appointed postmaster at Mills, February 5, 1889.

The route upon which these postoffices are located extends from Hagerstown to Mills. The mail is carried each way every day.

A postoffice was established at Rock Forge in 1894 and discontinued in the same year.

AGRICULTURAL DEVELOPMENT.

Limestone is the prevailing geological characteristic of the Antietam valley. This usually implies a soil of permanent and recuperative fertility, with the disadvantages of protruding rocks and uneven surface; but this description would not apply to the whole of Leitersburg District, although it is situated entirely within the watershed of the Antietam. The limestone also appears in combination with shale, sandstone, etc., and in many areas of considerable extent it is depressed far below the surface. In the western part of the District there is an extensive and fertile region locally known as the Marsh or Longmeadows. Here

SOCIAL AND MATERIAL DEVELOPMENT. 69

a black loam appears in many places as the principal constituent of the soil and while the surface is rolling, its elevations are everywhere gradual, thus imparting to the landscape a peculiar softness of contour. This locality may well be compared with the midland counties of England or the Blue Grass region of Kentucky. At the period of its first settlement the District was probably well timbered throughout its entire extent. Trees of various kinds—red oak, white oak, Spanish oak, wild cherry, locust, walnut, etc.—are referred to in the original land patents. When Mason and Dixon's Line was surveyed they employed a force of axemen to cut a vista through the forest. In 1770 Dr. Henry Schnebley purchased from Peter Shiess a tract of 713 acres, located principally in the District, to which he gave the name of The Forest, which certainly implies that it was well timbered. Scant Timber, the name of a tract patented by Wendell Sights in 1766, is equally suggestive.

The removal of the forest was the first concern of the pioneer. This was a laborious undertaking, without any compensation except the increased value of the land, as timber was not a marketable commodity. Sometimes the trees were "girdled," a process which consisted in the removal of a girdle of bark from the trunk, resulting in the death of the tree and the decay of the bark and branches, which fell to the ground and added greatly to its fertility.

The agricultural implements at the disposal of the pioneer * were few in number and of the crudest description. The plow

---

* Some idea of the equipment of a Leitersburg District farm and household in the colonial period may be gained from the following inventories of appraisement:

1755, Robert Downing: Twenty-six horses, 33 cattle, 41 hogs, 17 sheep, 4 bee-hives, sickles, augers, chisels, adze, axes, 1 still, still-tubs, barrels and half-barrels, tight hogsheads, grind-stone, cross-cut saw, grubbing hoes, spade, 1 iron harrow, 2 ploughs and irons, 1 wagon; 5 spinning wheels, 1 dough-tray, butter-tubs, 2 looking glasses, knives and forks, " pewter dishes, basins, plates, and spoons," iron pots, earthenware, smoothing-irons, 1 churn and cooler, "a clock and glass."

1764, Jacob Leiter: Eight horses, 7 cows, 4 sheep, 3 hogs, 1 cutting-box and knife, 1 iron harrow, 2 forks, 1 plow and plow-irons, 1 wagon, 1 grindstone, 1 cross-cut saw, 1 brass kettle, 1 still, stilling vessels, 4 grubbing hoes; 2 spinning wheels, 1 peppermill, 1 iron stove, "a parcel of pewter dishes and plates," 1 clock, 1 brass kettle, 1 iron kettle, "large Bible, hymn book, and a parcel of other books."

1776, George Hartle: Eight horses, 11 cattle, 11 hogs, 14 sheep, 1 iron harrow, 1 mill for cleaning grain, 1 old wagon, 1 grindstone, 2 mattocks, 1 sprouting hoe, 1 garden hoe, 2 weeding hoes, 1 broad-ax, 1 spade, 2 shovels, 1 brass scythe, 2 axes, 4 forks, 1 branding iron, "plow irons"; 1 weaver's loom and stays, 1 iron stove, 1 clock, "pewter basins, dishes, and plates," pewter spoons, 1 brass ladle, 1 iron kettle, "iron spoons, ladles, and water buckets," "1 large Bible," "books of different sorts."

with which the soil was first broken was made almost exclusively of wood. Wheat was sown broadcast; hay was cut with a scythe and raked by hand; grain was cut with a sickle and threshed with a flail. In the last century farming implements, like wearing apparel and household goods in general, were all of local manufacture. The iron forks used in handling manure, grain, and hay were made by the blacksmith; the prongs were half an inch thick at the base, tapered to a point, and the handle, which was inserted in the socket, was made by the farmer from a suitable sapling. For a shaking-fork a forked limb was cut from a tree, and its selection sometimes involved a long excursion through the forest. Plow-making was an art that had its special practitioners. In one day a skillful plow-maker could cut down a tree and from its materials fashion the beam, post, handles, mould-board, and landside, which, with the necessary irons, constituted the completed plow. Covering the mouldboard with sheet iron was an important improvement; others followed, eventually resulting in the evolution of the modern plow.

Cutting a harvest with the sickle was laborious and protracted. A good reaper could cut and bind an acre a day. Reapers generally worked in pairs and cut from one end of the field to the other; when the end opposite the starting point was reached one walked back some distance and carried both sickles while the other bound both swaths; he then laid down the sickles and bound both swaths until his companion overtook him, when it was again his turn to carry the sickles. The grain cradle was the first great improvement in harvesting facilities and the next was the reaping machine. In 1856 George Bell purchased a McCormick reaper and used it successfully in cutting his crop and that of his brother, Daniel Bell; this was the first introduction of harvesting machinery in Leitersburg District. It was drawn by four horses; the cutting apparatus and the reel were similar to those generally in use at the present day; the wheat was received upon a platform, from which the sheaves were raked off by a man who sat behind the master wheel. A year or two later the Manny machine was introduced; in this a man on the platform pushed off the wheat with a fork. The automatic rake soon followed and finally the automatic binder, the crowning feature of the harvester of the present day.

SOCIAL AND MATERIAL DEVELOPMENT. 71

When grain was threshed with a flail or tramped out by horses, this was a long and disagreeable task. The first threshing machine was merely an inclosed cylinder, from which the straw was removed and shaken with a fork. (Hence the word "shaking-fork.") With this primitive machine it was possible to thresh two hundred bushels in a day, after which about the same length of time was required to separate the wheat from the chaff with a wind-mill. The shaker, revolving fan, and straw carrier were successively devised, and threshing machines combining these were manufactured by John Dayhoff at Rock Forge and also by George Frick at a foundry located within the original limits of Leitersburg District. This foundry was removed to Waynesboro, Pa., in 1860, and eventually developed into the extensive plant of The Frick Company, capitalized at one million dollars.

When grain was sown broadcast it was covered with a harrow or shovel plow. The first grain drill had a rigid shovel fastened with a wooden pin, which broke when a stump or rock or other obstruction was encountered; as such occurrences were frequent a box of pins always accompanied the drill, to be inserted in place of those broken. Drills of this description were in use in Leitersburg District as early as 1850. Henry F. Bell manufactured grain drills at Waynesboro, Pa., from 1852 to 1857, in which the feeding device was a series of rotating cups and the shovel had a spring adjustment; these were the first drills of this kind manufactured and introduced in this locality. The drill rapidly superseded broadcast sowing.

The invention and improvement of the mower was contemporaneous with that of the reaper. The horse-rake, another important implement in connection with the hay crop, was at first a clumsy contrivance, in which the rake consisted of a wooden beam with two sets of wooden teeth projecting in opposite directions. The operator walked behind and manipulated the machine with a lever; when he lifted this one set of teeth dumped and the other set came into play. Henry Schriver purchased one of the first iron-tooth horse-rakes used in the District. With this machine the operator stood on the teeth to keep them down and raised them with a lever which he pushed with his foot. The first hand-lever spring-tooth rakes introduced in the District were manufactured by John Dayhoff at Rock Forge, and the first rake of this description that he sold was purchased by Samuel Martin in 1860.

The first centrifugal cream separator in Washington County was purchased in 1891 by Samuel Newcomer and placed in operation on his farm, which is situated partly in Leitersburg District and partly in Cavetown. It was manufactured by the De Laval Separator Company of New York. . In 1895 the Maugansville Creamery Association established a skimming station at Strite's mill near Leitersburg. The plant consisted of a Reid separator of large capacity driven by a steam engine. Its operation was continued at intervals for several years and then abandoned, owing to lack of patronage.

As the price of land is generally regarded as a fair index to agricultural development and prosperity, some statistics of this nature may not be inappropriate here. When the District was first settled land was purchased from the Proprietary at the uniform price of one shilling per acre, subject to an annual quit rent of four shillings per hundred acres and an equal amount upon every alienation thereof. Among the transfers of real estate prior to 1800 were the following: 1749, Thomas Cresap to Michael Miller, 260 acres, £220; 1755, George Poe to Christopher Burkhart, 173 acres, £15; 1762, George Poe to Jacob Leiter, 362 acres, £397; 1767, Peter Shiess to Peter Bell, 248 acres, £70; 1769, Peter Good to John Gabby, 166 acres, £400; 1770, Peter Shiess to Dr. Henry Schnebley, 713 acres, £100; 1773, Frederick Haldimand to Joseph Sprigg, 4,313 acres, £5,250; 1775, John Reiff to Christian Lantz, 476 acres, £2,350; 1779, Joseph Sprigg to Samuel Hughes, 1,300 acres, £21,000; 1779, Joseph Sprigg to John McConkey, 521 acres, £3,126; 1780, John McConkey to John Rench, 521 acres, £20,000; 1787, Jacob Good to Joseph Long, 350 acres, £1,800; 1795, Joseph Long to John Barr, 366 acres, £5,055.

Public Roads.

In the material and social development of the District public roads have been an important factor.

The judicial records of Frederick County afford but meager information regarding the early public roads of Antietam and Salisbury Hundreds, in which Leitersburg District was embraced. The first roads were doubtless bridle-paths, winding around the

SOCIAL AND MATERIAL DEVELOPMENT.

hills and avoiding the marshes; when it became necessary to widen these for wagon transportation the work was done by public cooperation, without the formality of legal proceedings. Hence the information of the court regarding the courses or even the termini of the earliest roads was exceedingly meager. Supervisors were regularly appointed, however, as shown in the following lists:

"All the main roads in Antietam Hundred:" 1749, Robert Turner; 1750, William Kelly; 1752-53, Isaac Hoser; 1754, John Carr; 1755, George Moore.

"All the main roads above Beaver creek in Antietam Hundred:" 1758-60, George Lambert; 1761, John Charlton; 1763, John Rohrer; 1766, Peter Fugate; 1768, James Walling; 1769-70, Henry Wall.

"All the main roads * * * from Baker's to Stull's mill, between that road and the Temporary Line in Salisbury Hundred:" 1749, John William Smith.

"From Baker's to Stull's mill, between that road and the Temporary Line in Salisbury Hundred, and from Aaron Price's to the Temporary Line, known by the name of 'The Old Road:'" 1750, Peter Rench; 1751, Conrad Hogmire; 1753, John Keller; 1754-55, Joseph Volgemore (Wolgamot); 1758, John Ritter; 1759, James Downing; 1760, Peter Dizer; 1761, Jacob Brumbaugh; 1763, Nicholas Martin; 1766, Samuel Pawling; 1768-69, Dilman Washabaugh.

"From Nicholson's Gap to Jacob Funk's mill and from said mill to Sharpsburg:" 1768, Conrad Hogmire; 1769-70, Samuel Grebill.

"The new road from the mouth of Conococheague through Elizabeth-Town to where it intersects the run below Haldimand's plantation:" 1770, Henry Tice.

At November sessions, 1749, of the Frederick County court, Jonathan Hager, Captain Thomas Prather, and Joseph Swearingen were appointed to view a proposed road "from the mouth of Conococheague to Stoner's mill on Antietam as far as the line extends." As Stoner's mill was situated at the present site of B. F. Welty's, one mile southeast of Waynesboro, this road would certainly have passed through Leitersburg District; but it does not appear that it was ever opened.

The earliest positive evidence of a road in Leitersburg

District that the writer has discovered occurs in the patent for Cousin's Obligement, a tract of fifty-one acres now embraced partly in the farm of Henry M. Jacobs near Miller's church and formerly owned for many years by Abraham Strite. This tract was patented to Andrew Hoover, February 14, 1755; its boundaries are described as "Beginning at a bounded walnut tree standing on the east side of the road that leads from Robert Downing's to George Burkhart's and among a parcel of limestone rocks by a large sink-hole." The house in which Downing lived still stands on the farm of Daniel N. Scheller near Ziegler's mill. It is difficult to identify Burkhart's residence, unless that of Christopher Burkhart is meant; in 1755 he lived on Antietam, where Samuel Martin now resides.

At that point in the South mountain where Mason and Dixon's Line crosses it there is a depression known at the middle of the last century and for many years thereafter as Nicholson's Gap. Of all the gaps in this range from the Potomac to the Susquehanna it is doubtful if any other possesses equal importance for commercial purposes. Here the Western Maryland railroad, the most important line of communication between the Cumberland valley and Baltimore, crosses the mountain barrier, and in the same vicinity may be seen the embankments and bridges of the old "Tape Worm" railroad, projected by Thaddeus Stevens in the '30's and partially constructed for many miles through Adams and Franklin Counties.

Nicholson's Gap was the focal point of several important public roads before the close of the colonial period. In 1761 a petition was presented to the court of quarter sessions of Cumberland County, Pa., by citizens of Peters Township, representing, "That they have no prospect for a standing market for the produce of their county only at Baltimore, and having no road leading from their township to said town of Baltimore, and flour being the principal commodity this township produceth," etc., and therefore praying the court to appoint viewers to lay out a road in the direction of Baltimore as far as the Temporary Line. Viewers were accordingly appointed, and at April sessions, 1768, they reported in favor of a road "crossing the Conococheague creek at the mouth of Muddy run, thence through Antrim Township to the gap commonly called Nicholson's in the South mountain"—

JACOBS CHURCH.

SOCIAL AND MATERIAL DEVELOPMENT.

the present route of the Mercersburg, Greencastle, and Waynesboro turnpike.*

Influenced doubtless by the same considerations the people of Antietam and Salisbury Hundreds were also making an effort at the same time to secure a legal road through Nicholson's Gap. Viewers were appointed by the Frederick County court at November sessions, 1767, and a year later their report was submitted. This document, with the action of the court relative thereto, reads as follows:

November Sessions, 1768.—Messrs. John Rohrer and Conrad Hogmire report to the court here as follows, viz.:

In obedience to an order of Frederick County November court, 1767, we, the subscribers, have viewed the several roads therein mentioned and find that a road from Nicholson's Gap may be made in a direct line to Jacob Funk's mill on Antietam and from thence through Sharpsburg to Swearingen's ferry on Potomac river with much more advantage to the public than any roads hitherto made, and we have given the proprietors notice on whose lands the said roads go through.

Also, we have carefully viewed the roads from the mouth of Opeckon ford leading a direct course to the chapel in All Saint's parish and from thence to Jacob Funk's mill on Antietam creek; and from Thatcher's ford on Potomac river to Ebersole's and Wolgamot's mills on the Great Marsh; and that all those roads can be laid out in a direct course with great advantage to the public, and have also given the proprietors notice on whose lands the said roads go through.

Witness our hands this 16th March, 1768.

JOHANNES ROHRER.
CONRAD HOGMIRE.

To the Worshipful Justices of Frederick County Court.

Upon reading which report the court concurs with the former part thereof; the latter is disallowed.

This is the road "from Nicholson's Gap to Jacob Funk's mill and from said mill to Sharpsburg" for which Conrad Hogmire was appointed supervisor in 1768. It passes through Fiddlersburg, crosses the Antietam at the Old Forge, and passes Beard's church and Welty's church. It was the original eastern boundary of Leitersburg District and still constitutes the extreme southeastern limit of its extent.

---

* McCauley's History of Franklin County, p. 133.

The following entry occurs in the minutes of the Frederick County court at November session, 1770:

> Joseph Gaither and sundry others prefer to the court here the following petition, to wit: "The humble petition of the inhabitants of Conococheague to the Worshipful Bench of Frederick County now sitting beg leave to inform you that there was a road led from the mouth of Conococheague to Nicholson's Gap, but at present it is quite useless; your petitioners therefore humbly beg that your Worships will be pleased to grant an order that the public road shall lead from the mouth of Conococheague through Elizabeth-Town until it intersects the road that leads through said gap, and they as in duty bound will pray." Joseph Gaither, Joseph Mitchell, and sundry others.
>
> Upon reading which petition and consideration thereon had it is ordered by the court here that Messrs. Colonel Thomas Prather, Van Swearingen, Jr., and Patrick Allison view and lay out the said road and make report thereof to the next court.

No report appears in the court minutes, but at the same term of court Henry Tice was appointed supervisor for "The new road from the mouth of Conococheague through Elizabeth-Town to where it intersects the run below Haldimand's plantation." Haldimand's plantation was the extensive Longmeadows tract; the new road therefore terminated at Marsh run at or near the Ziegler mill. But it was at this point that the road referred to in the patent for Cousin's Obligement (1755) began; hence it is highly probable that the latter continued to Nicholson's Gap. It had not yet became a legal road to that point in 1776, and as the records of the Washington County court for many years after the organization of the county are no longer in existence, it is impossible to say when this occurred.

There can be no uncertainty, however, regarding its course. On the 20th of December, 1790, the Legislature passed an act authorizing resurveys on a number of important roads in different parts of the State, one of which was the road "from Elizabeth-Town to the Pennsylvania line in Nicholson's Gap." Ludwig Young, William Lee, and Joseph Sprigg, Jr., were appointed as commissioners to make the resurvey, a report of which, signed by Messrs. Young and Lee under date of October 17, 1791, is entered in the land records of Washington County. This report shows the courses and distances of the road from the court house in Hagerstown (which then stood in the center of the public square) to the State line in Nicholson's Gap.*

The original course and changes made by the commissioners are both indicated. The alterations were very inconsiderable, and did not affect the general course of the road, which was originally thirteen miles and twelve perches in length and as amended eighty-five perches shorter. The only points indicated are Rench's mill, now owned by David Ziegler; Christian Leiter's, now the property of the estate of the late Joseph Strite; "Antietam at the Rock Forge;" and Frederick Howard's, near the present residence of Jacob Tharpe, about two hundred yards from the northeastern corner of the District on the State line. Its course seems to be identical with that of the road referred to in the patent for Cousin's Obligement (1755).

The resurvey of 1790 was evidently unsatisfactory to many interested parties, probably because its principal purpose—a direct road from Hagerstown to Nicholson's Gap—had not been accomplished. Accordingly, on the 15th of January, 1799, the Legislature passed a law repealing the act of December 2, 1790, so far as it applied to the Nicholson's Gap road. The levy court of Washington County was authorized to appoint "three discreet persons, freeholders in said county" as commissioners to lay out and survey

---

*Rev. Philip V. Fithian, a Presbyterian clergyman, passed over this road, May 18 1775, and thus describes it in his journal: "Here we arrived late last night at a small log house. A smart, neat, young land-lady, a spry, golden-haired, buxom maid, several sturdy wagoners, huge hills on every side—we are at what is called Nicholson's Gap. We jog on over the rugged hills. A middle-aged, dropsical Dutch woman with her face muffled up in the mumps boiled up for our breakfast a little coffee in the sugar and milk; indeed, it made good broth. From the mountain to Elizabeth or Hagerstown is a level country and good land."

Interesting allusions to the old road also occur in the following advertisements, which were published in the Washington [County] *Spy*:

Lost, on the night of the 14th inst. between Hagerstown and Burkhart's tavern on the road leading through Nicholson's Gap, a leather pocket book containing three notes * * * Whoever delivers said book and papers to me, living on Antietam near Burkhart's mill, shall receive the above reward. HENRY SNELL.
February 21, 1794.

Strayed or stolen from the subscriber, living on the main road leading from Hagerstown to Nicholson's Gap about two miles from Burkhart's mill, on the 19th of this inst. a black horse eight years old, fifteen hands high, shod before, branded on the near shoulder thus, C. G.; also a sorrel horse two years old last spring with a blazed face, branded on the near shoulder C * * * Any person taking up the said horses and bringing them to me shall receive $10.00 reward and reasonable charges paid by me. CHRISTIAN GARVER.
October 21, 1794.

a road "from Elizabeth-Town * * * * to Nicholson's Gap * * * * not exceeding forty feet in width, clear of ditches and in as straight lines as the nature of the ground * * * * will admit of." Unfortunately, the records of the levy court for this period have disappeared and it is therefore impossible to trace the proceedings under this law. But there can be no doubt that commissioners were duly appointed and that they proceeded to survey and open a road, visible and tangible evidence of which still exists after the lapse of nearly a century. On the farm of Immanuel and Kate E. Martin near Pleasant Hill school house there is a tract of woodland through which a vista forty feet wide extends in a northeast and southwest direction. Seventy years ago an almost unbroken forest extended from Leitersburg to Ringgold and there are persons still living who remember when the vista through the Martin woods was continuous for several miles. There can be no doubt that it was cut out in 1799 or 1800 as the course of the Nicholson's Gap road. Notwithstanding the expense thus incurred legislative interposition was again secured in the passage of the following act on the 31st of December, 1801:

A Supplement to an Act entitled, "An Act respecting the public Roads in Washington County," passed at November sessions, 1798.

WHEREAS, By an act of Assembly to which this is a supplement the levy court of said county did appoint commissioners to lay out and survey a road from Elizabeth-Town in Washington County to the Pennsylvania line in Nicholson's Gap; and whereas the said commissioners did proceed to lay out and survey the said road and did survey and lay out the said road in different directions, one of which has been confirmed by the said court: which road, so confirmed by the said court, it is represented to this General Assembly by a large number of respectable inhabitants of said county is the most inconvenient and expensive and on the worst ground ; and whereas it is also represented to this General Assembly that if the present levy court of the said county had the power to reject, alter, change, or confirm the said road, it would be highly beneficial to the inhabitants of the said county: therefore,

2. *Be it enacted by the General Assembly of Maryland,* That the justices of the levy court of Washington County be and they are hereby authorized and empowered to reject, alter, change, or confirm the said road so as aforesaid confirmed by the former levy court, and they are hereby authorized and empowered to confirm, reject, alter, or change either of the said routes as surveyed and laid out by the commissioners appointed under the act to which this is a supplement, or to lay out a new road in the discretion aforesaid;

SOCIAL AND MATERIAL DEVELOPMENT. 81

and the justices of the levy court are authorized and empowered to appoint commissioners for any or either of the purposes aforesaid, which commissioners when appointed shall have the powers and be subject to all the limitations given by the original act.

3. *And be it enacted*, That all the powers given to the supervisor or supervisors for the said road by the former levy court be and the same are hereby suspended, and he or they shall not proceed to clear or open the said road or any part thereof.

Under this act and doubtless in the next year (1802) the question of location was finally settled by the selection of the present course, which is that of the turnpike from Hagerstown to Leitersburg and the county road from Leitersburg through Ringgold toward the mountain.

The road from Greencastle to Smithsburg, the second public road opened through Leitersburg District, was authorized by an act of the Legislature passed on the 3d of January, 1807. It is described as leading "from the State line near Peter Baker's to intersect the main road leading from Hagerstown to Baltimore through Charlton's Gap at the foot of the South mountain near Robert Hughes's." William Gabby, Robert Hughes, and Jacob Rench constituted the commission under whose direction the survey was made. The only points indicated in Leitersburg District are Michael Wolfinger's (now the residence of Mrs. Joseph Strite), Russell's gate (Strite's mill), Antietam, Andrew Bachman's (east of Leitersburg), and Moyer's mill (now owned by George H. Bowman).

On the 6th of January, 1810, the Legislature passed a law opening to the public "a road from Hagerstown to the Pennsylvania line in the direction of Waynesboro"—the Marsh turnpike. A private road to the various residences along its course had been used by the public for many years but there were gates at the boundary of every farm, the removal of which was doubtless one of the main advantages to be gained in having it declared a public road. William O. Sprigg, through whose extensive estate the road passed for some distance, objected to this, and through his influence the law was repealed on the 24th of December, 1810. The road thus reverted to its original status and so continued for sixteen years. In 1824 a petition was addressed to the county court stating that it was "out of repair" and "at all seasons of the year almost impassable." Jacob Schnebley, John Harry, and Daniel Malott were accordingly appointed examiners, November 15, 1824. In their report, certified under date of November 11, 1825, they state that they proceeded "to locate the present road as it is now used, commencing at the Pennsylvania line and ending at its intersection with the Nicholson's Gap road." At March term, 1826, this report was confirmed, and thus the Marsh road was opened to the public. Two important changes have since been made in its course, one in 1839, by which the present location between Reid postoffice and the Pennsylvania line was established, and the other in 1869 at Paradise school house.

At April term, 1826, upon petition of Abraham Schmutz and others, the levy court appointed Henry Fouke, Jacob Huyett, and John Harry commissioners to lay out a road "from the Hagerstown and Nicholson's Gap road at or near Abraham Schmutz's mill across to the road leading from Hagerstown to Greencastle." The proposed road was accordingly surveyed under their direction, May 29, 1826; they reported "that the public convenience required the said road to be opened, on account of a private road being shut up" and that "a road is necessary for the convenience of the inhabitants of that section of the country to get to the mill." It was accordingly confirmed by the court at March term, 1827. This road constitutes the western boundary of Leitersburg District between Paradise school house and Ziegler's mill.

The following entry occurs in the proceedings of the levy court of Washington County under date of September 7, 1830:

Ordered by the court that the commission and return in the case of the commission issued to John Welty, Peter Mong, and Christopher Flory to open a road from Leitersburg to the Pennsylvania line above the place commonly called the Rock Forge be returned to said commissioners for amendment pursuant to the order of Washington County court passed in the said case.

The opening of this road was opposed by Robert Hughes, through whose lands it passed. The final survey was made on the 20th of July, 1831, by Benjamin Garver under the direction of Christopher Flory and Peter Mong, who laid out a road thirty-three feet wide extending from the public square in Leitersburg two miles and forty-four perches to the termination of a road already laid out from Waynesboro to the State line. It was confirmed by the county commissioners on the 8th of September,

SOCIAL AND MATERIAL DEVELOPMENT.

1831. This is the present course of the turnpike between Leitersburg and Waynesboro.

"Commencing at the Leitersburg and Waynesboro road at a private road that leads to Samuel Lyday's saw-mill; to continue to the Pennsylvania and Maryland line to a place called Jacobs meeting house; then northward to the land of Schriver and Horst; then the most direct route to the Leitersburg and Greencastle road, to terminate at a place commonly called Strite's hemp patch:" the road thus described was surveyed by Marmaduke W. Boyd, December 28, 1842, under the direction of George Poe, Daniel South, and Jacob Adams, examiners appointed by the county commissioners. There was dissatisfaction with the route selected, however, and a new board of examiners was appointed, composed of George Poe, James Coudy, and Emory Edwards, for whom Mr. Boyd surveyed the road from Jacobs church to the turnpike on the 7th of August, 1843. The entire line was confirmed by the county commissioners in 1845. This is the present public road from the turnpike at Rock Forge, past Jacobs church, across the Greencastle road, past Miller's church, to the turnpike near Mt. Union school house.

From the Leitersburg and Waynesboro road to Flagg's crossing, thence to Funk's mill, and thence to Henry Schriver's—this road was surveyed by Benjamin Garver, June 9, 1848, for a board of examiners composed of himself, Abraham Strite, and Jacob E. Bell. It was confirmed with a width of thirty feet in 1850, but the course was materially changed between the first survey and the final confirmation. This road diverges from the turnpike about half a mile north of Leitersburg, crosses the Antietam, passes New Harmony school house, and terminates at the road from Jacobs to Miller's church.

A short distance east of Jacob's church a road diverges to the south, terminating at the property of Benjamin Baker as originally laid out. This road was surveyed by Benjamin Garver, April 26, 1850, and confirmed with a width of twenty-five feet. Henry Schriver and Robert Fowler were associated with Mr. Garver as examiners.

The road from New Harmony school house to the Greencastle road was surveyed by Benjamin Garver, October 24, 1850, and subsequently confirmed with a width of twenty-five feet. The examiners were Benjamin Garver and George Poe.

The public road from the turnpike near Mt. Union school house to the Old Forge road, a distance of one and three-eighths miles, was surveyed by Benjamin Garver, March 15, 1850, and confirmed in 1851 with a width of twenty-five feet. The examiners were Joseph Garver, Andrew M. Shank, and Abraham Strite.

From "Antietam bridge near Fowler & Ziegler's mill past David Brumbaugh's mill to the old Marsh road," a distance of two miles and 184 perches—this road was surveyed by John Oswald, September 15-16, 1852, under the direction of Samuel Etnyer, Peter Bell, and Jacob H. Barr, examiners. It was confirmed in 1853 with a width of twenty-five feet. The "Antietam bridge" referred to is on the turnpike a short distance southwest of Leitersburg, and "David Brumbaugh's mill" is now owned by Henry F. Lehman.

About a mile northeast of Leitersburg a road 158 perches in length connects the Waynesboro turnpike and the Ringgold road. It was surveyed on the 26th of December, 1854, and confirmed in 1855 with a width of twenty-four feet. The examiners were Jacob E. Bell, Henry Schriver, and George Beard.

The public road from Martin's school house to Welty's church, which constitutes the eastern line of Leitersburg District for some distance, was surveyed by John Oswald, September 13, 1852, "upon or near the old road now in use by the neighborhood." The examiners were David Oswald, Jeremiah S. Besore, and Elijah Bishop. This road was confirmed in 1853 with a width of twenty-five feet.

The public road that forms the eastern boundary of the District from the Ringgold road to Charles's mill was surveyed by John Oswald, November 15, 1853. The examiners were Frederick Bell, Peter Bell, and George Kessinger. The authorized width of this road is twenty feet.

From the Smithsburg road near Bowman's mill a road diverges to the Old Forge road. It was surveyed on the 23d of October, 1858, and confirmed in the following month. The examiners were George Poe, Henry Schriver, and John Welty. The authorized width is thirty feet.

The road from the turnpike to the Antietam at Henry Hartle's was surveyed by S. S. Downin, December 26, 1868, and confirmed in 1870. The examiners were I. G. Brown and William B. Strock.

SOCIAL AND MATERIAL DEVELOPMENT.

It was originally designed to continue this road to the Old Forge, and a resurvey for this purpose, made in 1897 by E. E. Piper and confirmed by the county commissioners, is now in litigation.

A road 158.43 perches in length extending from the Greencastle road to the Pennsylvania line was surveyed by S. S. Downin, June 10, 1872, and confirmed in December of the same year. The examiners were John F. Lehman, John D. Eakle, and Joseph Middlekauff.

The road from Buena Vista school house on the Old Forge road by way of "the watery lane" to the Leitersburg and Smithsburg road, which constitutes the eastern line of the District for some distance, was surveyed by P. Oswald, June 11, 1875, and confirmed in September of the same year. The examiners were Isaac E. Davis, Edward Ingram, and Joseph Kimler.

A road 295 perches in length extending eastward from the Ringgold road to the eastern line of the District was surveyed by E. E. Piper, February 4. 1891, and subsequently confirmed. The examiners were John Martin, Jr., William H. Rohrer, and Isaac G. Beard.

In 1811 there were three public road districts in Leitersburg District, described as follows: No. 20.—"The road from Hagerstown by Rench's mill to Antietam creek below Lantz's mill on the Nicholson's Gap road: six miles." No. 21.—"The road from Lantz's fording on the Nicholson's Gap road to the Pennsylvania line: six miles." No. 22.—"The road from the Pennsylvania line near Peter Baker's until it intersects the Charlton's Gap road near Robert Hughes's: seven miles." The respective supervisors were Christopher Trovinger, John Mentzer, and Michael Wolfinger. The appropriation for No. 20 was $100.00; for No. 21, $60.00; for No. 22, $80.00.

In 1812 the levy court established the following rates of pay for work on the county roads:

A wagon, four horses, and driver.	$2 67
A wagon, two horses, and driver.	1 67
A cart, two horses or oxen, and driver.	1 67
A cart, one horse, and driver,	1 34
An able-bodied man,	75
An able-bodied man with wheelbarrow.	80
A plough, two horses, and driver.	1 34
An able-bodied man engaged in blowing rocks,	1 00

Various changes have been made and other methods have been tried, but the system of road construction and repair in Washington County is substantially the same as in 1811 and for many years previous to that date. The public roads are divided into districts, for each of which a supervisor is appointed and an appropriation made from the county treasury. Special improvement by private initiative is encouraged, however; where the supervisor or other interested citizens express a willingness to bestow labor or materials gratis in the construction of permanent improvements the county commissioners usually reward their enterprise by an increased appropriation. In this way two of the steepest hills on the Smithsburg road southeast of Leitersburg were reduced to much better grades in 1897-98, largely through the efforts of Freeland W. Anderson and Dr. J. H. Wishard; and in 1897 Samuel Cook and John F. Strite hauled 155 loads of stone on the Greencastle road adjacent to the Pennsylvania line, with which it was macadamized for a considerable distance. In both instances the county commissioners granted liberal appropriations in aid of the work.

Horseback riding was once the universal mode of travel. Wagons were used in hauling grain, merchandise, etc., but no vehicle for personal transportation was known to the pioneers of Leitersburg District. On errands of pleasure or business everybody travelled on horseback. At funerals the coffin was placed on a farm wagon and a similar conveyance carried the family of the deceased, while the relatives and friends followed on horseback like a troop of cavalry. In many families the daughters as well as the sons had their riding horses, with the necessary equipment of saddle, bridle, etc. As the condition of the roads improved gigs, carriages, and other light vehicles with leather springs were introduced, but they differed greatly from the modern type both in comfort and appearance.

Before the construction of railroads grain, flour, whiskey, and other products were transported to market by wagon, and on many of the larger farms a six-horse team was employed in this way for several months every year. The shortest route from the District to Baltimore was the road through Nicholson's Gap, Mechanicstown, and Westminster, but in the winter and spring the journey was generally made by way of the National road through Middletown and Frederick. Seven days were required for the journey by way of Nicholson's Gap and eight days by way of Frederick.

In 1821 a line of stage coaches was established between Gettysburg and Hagerstown by way of Nicholson's Gap. It formed part of the line between Philadelphia and Wheeling. The coaches were drawn by four horses and Leitersburg was a point of exchange.

BRIDGES.

On the 14th of January, 1824, the Legislature passed an act authorizing the levy court of Washington County to erect a bridge over Antietam creek at Frederick Ziegler's ford on the Nicholson's Gap road; and on the 3d of May, 1824, the court entered into a contract with James Lloyd for the erection of a stone bridge at the point designated for the sum of $2,175. This is the bridge on the turnpike a short distance southwest of Leitersburg.

In 1838 the county commissioners were authorized to build "over Antietam creek upon the best practicable site at or near Lewis Ziegler's ford on the road leading from Greencastle to Baltimore a substantial stone bridge." It was accordingly erected in the following year by J. Weaver. This is the bridge directly west of Leitersburg on the Greencastle road.

In recent years the county commissioners have erected four iron bridges in the District, located as follows: on the Antietam at Rock Forge and at the crossing on the public road between that point and Leitersburg; on the Little Antietam at the crossing on the Chewsville road and at Bowman's mill.

TURNPIKES.

The Hagerstown and Antietam Turnpike Company was incorporated by the Maryland Legislature, February 2, 1819, "to make a turnpike road from the public square in Hagerstown to intersect the turnpike road leading from Gettysburg through Nicholson's Gap at the Pennsylvania line." Christopher Burkhart, Frederick Ziegler, John Welty, Joseph Gabby, Otho Holland Williams, and Upton Lawrence were designated as commissioners for the organization of the company. The authorized capital was $60,000. The company secured several extensions of its franchise, but it does not appear that the project ever passed the initial stage.

HISTORY OF LEITERSBURG DISTRICT.

On the 11th of March, 1840, the Legislature passed an act authorizing Robert M. Tidball, Charles A. Fletcher, Lewis Ziegler, Samuel Lyday, William E. Doyle, Dr. Frederick Dorsey, Abraham Strite, and Joseph Gabby to conduct a lottery for the purpose of raising a sum not exceeding $30,000 "to be applied to the making of a turnpike road from Hagerstown through Leitersburg to the Pennsylvania line, and for introducing wholesome water into the town of Leitersburg." It does not appear that the lottery was ever organized, although the commissioners held a meeting in Hagerstown for that purpose in 1840.

The Hagerstown and Waynesboro Turnpike Company was incorporated by the Maryland Legislature at December session, 1846, for the construction of "an artificial bed of stone or gravel not less than sixteen feet in breadth" on the bed of the county road "to be commenced at some point within the corporate limits of the town of Hagerstown and extended to the Pennsylvania line in the direction of Waynesboro through the town of Leitersburg." The act of incorporation authorized two toll gates and designated the rates of toll, which have been modified by subsequent legislation.

The corporators named in the charter were Joseph Gabby, Frederick Ziegler, Abraham Strite, Lewis Ziegler, John Mentzer, and Frederick Dorsey. The company organized on the 6th of May, 1847, by the election of the following officers: President, Abraham Strite; treasurer, Jacob E. Bell; managers, Nathan McDowell, Frederick Bell, Benjamin Garver, George L. Ziegler, and Christian Strite. The first secretary of the company was Benjamin Garver, who was elected on the 17th of May, 1847.

The road is nine miles in length, and was constructed under contract by Robert Fowler and Frederick K. Ziegler. On the 13th of June, 1847, a commission composed of Joseph Gabby, Abraham Strite, William E. Doyle, Lewis Ziegler, Samuel Lyday, and R. M. Tidball certified to the completion of three miles of road extending eastward from Hagerstown. The first toll collector at Gate No. 1 was Robert Bigham, who was appointed on the 1st of November, 1847. At Gate No. 2 the first collector was Jacob Garver; tolls were not collected here until November, 1848.

The capital stock of the company is issued in shares of $25.00 each. The amount originally subscribed was $10,260; this was insufficient for the construction of the road, however, and a considerable indebtedness was necessarily contracted. This was gradually liquidated out of the earnings of the road, after which the stock was increased by the amount of indebtedness thus paid. The present capital is $16,456.25, of which Washington County holds $2,500. No dividend was declared until 1861, all the surplus earnings of the road up to that date having been applied to the payment of indebtedness. Since 1861 dividends have been regularly declared, and the company's stock is regarded as a desirable investment.

The succession of presidents of the company since its organization has been as follows: 1847-49, Abraham Strite; 1850-53, Robert Fowler; 1854. George L. Ziegler; 1855-63, Abraham Strite; 1864-67, Jacob Miller; 1868-71, Daniel Mentzer; 1872, David M. Deitrich; 1873-95, David Strite; 1896-97, Alexander Neill.

The following persons have served as secretaries of the company: 1847, Benjamin Garver; 1848-49, Christian Strite; 1850, David M. Good; 1851-53, George L. Ziegler; 1854-72, Frederick Bell; 1873-83, David M. Deitrich; 1884-97, Josephus Ground.

The succession of treasurers has been as follows: 1847, Jacob E. Bell, Joseph Leiter; 1848-50, Abraham Strite; 1851-54, Robert Fowler; 1855, Abraham Strite; 1856-58, Jacob Miller; 1859-63, Abraham Strite; 1863-85, George W. Pole; 1886-93, Samuel Strite; 1893-97, Josephus Ground.

The president of the company during the years of its early history usually performed the duties of superintendent. The incumbents of this office since 1865 have been as follows: 1865-68, Daniel Mentzer; 1869-71, David Strite; 1872, David M. Deitrich; 1873-79, David Strite; 1881-92, John Miller; 1893-97, Samuel Strite.

The Marsh Turnpike Company was incorporated by the Maryland Legislature at January session, 1868. The first directors were David Cleaver, Peter Middlekauff, Jacob Oberholtzer, Daniel G. Rowland, and Peter Eshleman, who organized on the 25th of March, 1870, by electing Peter Middlekauff president and Daniel G. Rowland secretary. Three hundred and forty-eight shares of stock (par value, $25.00) having been subscribed, the stockholders met at Paradise school house, April 2, 1870, when a permanent organization was effected, constituted as follows: Directors: Joseph Eshleman, Peter Middlekauff, Daniel G. Rowland, Daniel N. Scheller, and George A. Cressler; president, Peter Middlekauff; secretary, Peter Eshleman; treasurer, Henry Clopper. On the 22d of April, 1870, the contract for the construction of the turnpike was awarded to Michael Dillon at $2498 per mile; and on the 18th of March, 1871, the work of construction having been completed, he received final payment. The line of the road extends from the State line to the Hagerstown and Waynesboro turnpike, a distance of four miles.

The officers of the company since its organization have been as follows: Presidents: Peter Middlekauff, 1870-71; George A. Cressler, 1872-73; Jonas Eshleman, 1874-77; George A. Cressler, 1878-79; Joseph Eshleman, 1880-90; George A. Cressler, 1891-93; John H. Miller, 1894-98. Secretaries: Peter Eshleman, George A. Cressler, Jonas Eshleman, Peter R. Eshleman, Emanuel Burger. Treasurers: Henry Clopper, 1870-75; Peter R. Eshleman, 1876-77; Jonas Eshleman, 1878-81; George A. Cressler, 1882-90; Peter R. Eshleman, 1891-93; Jacob Eshleman, 1894-98.

MILLS.

Mills for grinding grain and sawing lumber were among the first necessities of a community and usually followed closely upon its settlement. Before the erection of a mill upon the territory of the District its inhabitants resorted to Stull's, on the Antietam near Hagerstown, which was built prior to 1748; Stoner's, which was in operation as early as 1749 on the Antietam east of Waynesboro at the present site of B. F. Welty's; or possibly to Wolgamot's on the Conococheague. But the water power afforded by the streams of the District offered ample inducement to local enterprise and was early utilized for commercial purposes.

As evidenced by Colonel Bouquet's will, there was a saw-mill on the Longmeadows estate in 1765. Its site was on the farm of Daniel N. Scheller, near the Marsh run and Paradise spring, where the wheel-pit may still be seen, the masonry of which is still in a good state of preservation. On the opposite side of the Marsh turnpike and on a branch of Marsh run is Snively's sawmill; it was from this branch that the power was derived and the course of the old race, extending from Snively's along the line between the lands of Lehman and Scheller, was clearly distinguishable some years ago.

SOCIAL AND MATERIAL DEVELOPMENT.

In 1772, as shown by the depositions in the Skipton-on-Craven boundary case, there was a saw-mill on the Little Antietam just below the bridge on the Chewsville road and opposite the present residence of Harvey J. Hartle. Nothing now remains to mark its site.

One of the first grist-mills in the District was that of Christopher Burkhart on Antietam creek a mile north of Leitersburg. The site is now embraced in the lands of Samuel Martin. It is probable that this mill was established as early as 1770. The erection of the mill-dam resulted injuriously to the lands of Peter Shiess, who resided on the opposite side of the creek, and in 1779 Burkhart purchased from him eleven and three-fourths acres of land, "together with all and singular the water and water courses, and all the drained lands, meadows, and other of the benefits of the waters stopped and gorged up by the damming of the water for the use of the above named Christopher Burkhart's grist-mills * * * and any other waters that may be stopped or gorged up by means of said Christopher Burkhart's mill-dam, for the benefit and advantage of said Burkhart and his mills in any kind or nature whatever." In 1797 Burkhart leased the mill, dwelling house, and lands adjacent thereto to Levan Hays for the term of seven years at an annual rental of £200. A "new mill-dam" recently erected is referred to in this lease. By his will, executed November 10, 1797, he devised the mill property to his son, Christopher Burkhart, in whose possession it continued until his death in 1838. Among those who operated it under lease from him were George Shiess and Samuel Lyday. After the property passed out of the possession of the Burkharts the successive owners were Henry Funk, Henry H. Snively, Daniel Mentzer, George Bell, and Christian Lehman. The old mill was a two-story stone structure, equipped at the close of its career with two sets of buhrs. This building was removed in 1857 by Daniel Mentzer, who erected on the same site a new mill that was regarded as one of the most commodious on Antietam creek. It was three stories high and the walls were built of stone to the second story. This building was completely destroyed by fire on the 29th of January, 1886. Only the foundation walls now remain to mark its site. There was also a saw-mill connected with this property at one time; it survived the period of its usefulness and after reaching an advanced stage of dilapidation was eventually removed. Christian Lantz seems to have formed the idea of erecting a mill soon after he became a resident of Leitersburg District, for in 1775 he purchased from Jacob Leiter two and one-half acres of land, the boundaries of which are described as "Beginning at the end of thirty-two perches in the sixth line of a tract of land called Skipton-on-Craven and running from thence down Antietam creek on the northwest side of said creek * * * to include the whole of the creek and all the advantages of the water for water works." The last clause is significant. In 1783 Lantz entered into an agreement with Leiter "not to raise the water or dam further or higher than the aforesaid corners or marked stones when there is not a flow in the creek, but at all other times he and his heirs and assigns are at liberty to raise the dam or water if they choose as far as the said stones but no farther, only when the flow is high." In a provisional disposition of his lands in 1792 Christian Lantz assigned the mill property to his son Christian and adjacent land to his son George, reserving to the latter "the use of the water every Monday night, Thursday night, and Saturday night forever, to be let through a hole made one foot square in the said Christian Lantz's mill race where George Lantz may think proper for the convenience of watering the said George Lantz's meadows."

The Lantz mill was situated west of Leitersburg on the opposite side of the Antietam creek and a short distance above the turnpike bridge over that stream. At the beginning of the century this crossing is referred to as "Lantz's fording on the Nicholson's Gap road." From Christian Lantz, Jr., the son of the first proprietor, the mill passed to his son-in-law, John Byer, by whom several other manufacturing establishments were also operated here. These included a saw-mill, tannery, hemp-mill, and distillery. Fowler & Ziegler subsequently bought the property, equipped the mill with new machinery, and transacted an extensive business, which rapidly declined after they discontinued operations.

On the south side of the turnpike at the point where Marsh run crosses the District line stands one of the oldest mills in Washington County. This mill is located on a draft of the Nicholson's

SOCIAL AND MATERIAL DEVELOPMENT.

Gap road in 1791 under the name of Rench's mill. It was built by John Rench, who purchased the site in 1780 in connection with a tract of over four hundred acres. He died in 1794 and by the terms of his will the mill was devised to his son, Peter Rench, by whose heirs it was sold in 1819 to Joseph Miller. The next owner was Abraham Schmutz, from whom the property passed to D. G. Yost and Adam Kinkle in 1826. On the 29th of June, 1833, Yost and Kinkle entered into an agreement with Frederick Ziegler for the sale of the mill and all its appurtenances, in consideration of which he agreed to deliver to them at Hagerstown "375 barrels of good, merchantable, first proof whiskey, to be the same quality of whiskey which the said Ziegler has been in the habit of selling in Baltimore, Georgetown, and other cities at from fifty to fifty-five cents per gallon." It was further stipulated that the capacity of the barrels should average thirty-four gallons. At this time (1833) the mill was operated under lease by Thomas Phillips. The property appears to have been in litigation about this time, as Ziegler did not secure a valid deed until 1847. At his death it passed to his son, David Ziegler, of Greencastle, Pa., in whose possession it has since remained. The present lessee is Samuel Hartman.

Some time near the close of the last century General Sprigg built a mill on Marsh run in the extreme northwestern part of the District. It was a two-story stone structure about forty feet square. The power was originally derived from a dam a half-mile distant. David Brumbaugh, who subsequently purchased the property, improved it in various ways and excavated a reservoir with an area of half an acre. Brumbaugh sold it to Jacob B. Lehman in 1854, and from him it was purchased in 1858 by his son, Henry F. Lehman, the present proprietor. The old stone mill was removed in 1869 and replaced by the main part of the present structure, a brick building thirty-eight by forty-five feet in dimensions, to which a frame addition thirty by thirty-one was added in 1878. Steam power was introduced in 1887, and at the present time engines of thirty-five horse-power are used. The use of buhrs in the manufacture of flour was discontinued in 1887 in favor of the roller process, to which the gyrator system of bolting was added in 1897. The present capacity of the mill is fifty barrels per day. It is also provided with facilities for the manufacture of other mill products, and in the character of its equipment and the extent of its business is justly regarded as one of the leading mills of Washington County.

An advertisement in the Washington *Spy* for May 3, 1793, refers to "Jacob Gilbert's mill, on Little Antietam creek, seven miles from Hagerstown and two miles off the main road leading from said town to Nicholson's Gap." Here Gilbert owned two hundred acres of land, which he purchased in 1789 from Abraham Stouffer, who is said to have built the mill. He derived his title from Christian Hyple. In 1800 Gilbert sold it to Abraham Moyer, by whom it was owned when the Smithsburg road was opened. He became insolvent and in 1825 the property was purchased at sheriff's sale by Frederick Bell, who built the present mill in 1837-38 and equipped it with new machinery throughout. He died in 1839 and in 1840 the mill was bought by his son, Frederick Bell. Among the subsequent owners were Samuel Etnyer, David M Deitrich, Jeremiah Fahrney, Elias R. Stottlemeyer, and George H. Bowman, the present proprietor, who purchased it in 1886. He introduced the roller process in 1896 and has also improved the property in various other ways.

Strite's mill near Leitersburg has been known by this name for more than half a century. The mill site and adjacent land were owned by the first Jacob Leiter at his death in 1764 and devised by him to his son, Christian. He sold it in 1790 to Peter Shanaberger, from whom it was purchased in 1792 by Samuel Kraumer (Cromer). While it is possible that some previous owner may have built and operated a mill at this site, there can be no doubt that the present structure was erected by Kraumer. A large stone in the front wall bears the inscription, "S. K. 1798." Further authentic testimony occurs in a deed from Jacob Leiter (of Peter) to Felix Beck for land subsequently owned by George Ziegler, the boundary of which is described as beginning at a tree on the west bank of the Antietam creek "two perches below Samuel Kraumer's mill house." This deed was executed in 1799. In 1807 Kraumer sold the property to John Russell, who was from the Shenandoah valley in Virginia. He died in 1808; his son, Christian Russell, by inheritance and purchase secured a two-thirds interest in the property, which he operated until 1829, when financial reverses compelled him to sell it. He then engaged in

SOCIAL AND MATERIAL DEVELOPMENT.

other business and eventually lost his life in a steamboat explosion on the Mississippi. Stephen Martin purchased the mill in 1829 and owned it until his death. It was bought in 1843 by Christian Strite, by whom the south wing was built for grinding plaster. He died in 1862, after which the property was purchased by Samuel Strite, the present owner. This is one of the largest mills on Antietam creek and is equipped throughout with modern machinery. The present lessee is John C. Strite.

Early in the century the Barr family built a mill on their estate in the eastern part of the District on Little Antietam. Here they conducted a variety of industrial operations. In one stone building there was a plaster-mill, saw-mill, and clover-mill, and in another a nail factory and distillery. The property was purchased in 1823 by Daniel Winter, whose son-in-law, Isaac H. Durboraw, was the next owner of the mill. The present proprietor is Rudolph Charles, who bought it in 1894. It is a substantial stone building. A short distance further down the creek is a saw-mill, owned by Jacob B. Stoner.

ROCK FORGE.

Great Rocks was a tract of fifty acres originally patented to Daniel Dulany on the 5th of April, 1750. The boundary is described as "Beginning at a bounded white oak standing near a spring called the Locust spring on the east side of Great Antietam about a mile from the Temporary Line." This spring is situated a short distance down the creek from the Rock Forge bridge. In 1769 Daniel and Walter Dulany of Annapolis, executors of Daniel Dulany, Sr., sold this tract to Lawrence O'Neal; and several years later it was purchased by Daniel Hughes.

Below the Locust spring the bank of the creek is quite steep; but the "great rocks" from which the tract derived its name are some distance above. Here the rocks rise precipitously at the southern bank of the creek and for some distance west of the present channel, which turns to the south at right angles with its former course and passes through a deep and narrow gorge. There is ample evidence that the creek originally described a circle of fully half a mile around the northern front and western slope of the rocky barrier through which it now passes. It is impossible to account for the immense deposits of sand on the farm of William Barkdoll on any other hypothesis; and when the creek overflows the waters still follow the old channel. If this view of the original course of the creek is correct, the gorge through which it passes must have been artificially excavated; and it was doubtless the practicability of such an excavation that attracted the attention of Colonel Hughes. There was probably a natural depression in the rocky barrier at this point, so that the undertaking was not so formidable as might appear; and it was further facilitated by the geological formation, which is that of strata inclined at an angle convenient for the operations of the quarryman.

While there can be no doubt that Colonel Hughes first developed the property for industrial purposes, the time when this was done is difficult to determine. In 1780 he married Susanna Schlatter and in lieu of dower in his extensive estate executed for her benefit a deed of trust to Samuel Purviance of Baltimore for Poor Robin's Almanac (213 acres), Great Rocks, and The Resurvey on Sarah's Delight ((770 acres) as security for the payment of an annuity of £150 to her in case she survived him. It is certainly highly improbable that Great Rocks would have been included in this deed if it had been the location of a valuable plant. Like the other tracts specified in the deed, it was probably unimproved land.

The earliest positive evidence of the existence of the forge that the writer has discovered occurs in the Maryland *Journal*, a newspaper publishd at Baltimore. The issue of this paper for March 31, 1786, contains the following advertisement:

To be rented: The Mt. Aetna Furnace, lying in Washington County, State of Maryland, and within six miles of Hagerstown. The ore is of excellent quality, either for bar iron or castings, which, with wood, limestone, and sand, is in great abundance and very convenient to the works. The buildings, bellows, gears, etc. are in good repair and the stream of water constant. Pot, stove, and other patterns may be had with the furnace, as also meadow ground and land for farming.

The Great Rock Forge is also to be rented; it stands on Antietam creek, within eight miles of the above furnace, has two hammers and four fires, a substantial dam, and considerable head of water. A lease may be given for three or seven years. For terms, apply to Daniel Hughes in Hagerstown.

DANIEL AND SAMUEL HUGHES.

March 23, 1786.

SOCIAL AND MATERIAL DEVELOPMENT.

The old forge was a substantial stone building, one story high, with two stone chimneys as high as the highest trees in the vicinity. It stood on the east side of the creek, opposite the present distillery of Benjamin Shockey and almost directly in front of the present residence of John Furnora, in whose property the site is now embraced. Here there is a narrow strip of meadow, the soil of which consists largely of ashes and other refuse from the old forge. The site of the dam is still plainly indicated by its ruins, which extend across the creek several rods below the present structure. During the period of its operation the plant probably employed a dozen workmen, while several teams were also required. The product* probably consisted principally of bar iron suitable for use by blacksmiths.

In 1805 Colonel Daniel Hughes entered into an agreement with Henry Jaccbs for the sale of "as much of the tract of land called Balsher's Misfortune as may lie on the north side of the State line and northwest of the Antietam creek, not to include any of the land that the Rock Forge dam formerly covered with water." This reference to the forge is significant. It shows that the dam had sustained material injury, in consequence of which it is fair to infer that the property was no longer operated. Colonel Hughes was interested in other iron plants, including Mt. Aetna Furnace, the Old Forge in Chewsville District, and Antietam Iron Works at the mouth of the Antietam, and to one of these the machinery was doubtless removed. He still seems to have retained some idea of rehabilitating the property, however: in his will, executed in 1809, he refers to "an iron estate by the name of Mt. Alto Furnace and the Rock Forge," in which his son Samuel held an equal interest with himself. But in 1811 they erected a blomary and forge on East Antietam creek in Franklin County, Pa., and this was operated in connection with the Mt. Alto Furnace. All idea of re-

---

*Cannon and cannon balls have been found in the *debris* at the site of the old forge, and it has been supposed that they were manufactured here. The Hugheses made cannon for the Maryland State troops during the Revolution, but so far as can be ascertained this was done at their works at the mouth of the Antietam. At the beginning of the century the land between the present course of the creek and its former channel was called Tory island, the origin of which would be difficult to explain as Colonel Hughes was an active and influential patriot. Another interesting story associated with the locality is the tradition of hidden treasure in the caves at the sides of the gorge.

sumption at Rock Forge was now abandoned. The old stone building fell into decay and each succeeding spring freshet left the dam in worse condition than before. Immense quantities of sand were hauled to Mt. Alto, but otherwise the property received but little attention from the Hugheses. It still possessed advantages that were not neglected by the public, however; above the old dam there was a wide, deep pool, and on summer Sundays horses were brought here from all the country around and made to plunge and swim. The old forge dam was sometimes the scene of animated equestrian performances.

In 1840 Holker Hughes sold the property to Samuel Lyday, and with this transfer its modern history begins. Lyday erected a dam at the present site and built the saw-mill; here he did a thriving business in sawing lumber for the United States gun factory at Harper's Ferry, W. Va. The finest walnut timber for miles around was secured for this purpose and entered into the construction of thousands of muskets afterward used in the Mexican War. In 1851 Lyday sold the property to Samuel Etnyer, from whom it was purchased by Jacob Tritle in the following year. He sold it in 1857 to John S. Dayhoff, and in his possession it continued until his death in 1876. Dayhoff built the machine shop, foundry, blacksmith shop, etc., and established an implement manufactory of considerable local importance. Grain separators, horse-powers, hay rakes, farm wagons, corn shellers, etc. were made here. In 1874-75 the plant was leased by Samuel Martin and George M. D. Bell. It was purchased in 1877 by Garver, Foltz & Company, who manufactured implements and transacted a general foundry and machine business. In 1882 they removed to Hagerstown and the property was subsequently converted into a distillery, of which the present proprietor is Benjamin Shockey.

Distilleries.

While the mills of the District have always been a prominent feature of its business and manufacturing interests, there was a time when they did not constitute the only local market for grain. Distilling was also a business of considerable importance. In proportion to its bulk whiskey was many times more valuable than flour, and as transportation was expensive and laborious it is not surprising that a large part of the cereal product of the District found its way to market through the still. The profits were also large, the plant did not usually involve a large investment of capital, and hence many men were engaged in the business.

The personal property of Robert Downing as appraised in 1755 included "one still, still tubs, barrels and half-barrels," etc. "One brass kettle, one still, and stilling vessels" are also mentioned in the inventory of Jacob Leiter's personality (1764). At that time and for many years thereafter the still was considered by many farmers a necessary part of farm equipment.

The following is believed to be a complete enumeration of the distilleries of the District: General Thomas Sprigg's, which was operated in a stone building at a spring between the mansion and the turnpike; Thomas Belt's, on the Colebrook farm, now owned by Isaac Shank, where the stone building in which it was operated stands between the house and barn; Michael Wolfinger's, on the Greencastle road at the present residence of Mrs. Catharine Strite; George Shiess's, of which he at one time operated three in Leitersburg District, located on the farms of Franklin M. Strite and Daniel Oller; Lewis Ziegler's, near Leitersburg, on the farm owned by the late David Strite; Joseph Gabby's, near the creek south of the house on the farm of Hiram D. Middlekauff; Frederick Ziegler's, on the farm of George F. Ziegler near Leitersburg; Andrew M. Shank's, on the farm of Immanuel and Kate E. Martin; Stephen Martin's, at the residence of Daniel W. Durborow; Fowler & Ziegler's, in succession to John Byer's, on the Antietam west of Leitersburg near the turnpike; Abraham Moyer's, at Bowman's mill; Michael Wolfinger's, on Water street in Leitersburg; and in recent years Jacob Wishard's on the farm of Freeland W. Anderson and Benjamin Shockey's at Rock Forge.

Frederick Ziegler engaged in the distilling business about 1810. His first distillery was a small one-story building near the large stone mansion on the pike west of Leitersburg, but about the year 1835 he built a stone structure on the opposite side of the road and here he continued the business for some years. This was considered one of the best equipped distilleries in the District at that date. The product was hauled to Frederick, Md., and Georgetown, D. C., for shipment to the cities, where it was sold through commission merchants and enjoyed a high reputation. Every barrel was branded with the letter "O" between the first and second hoops.

The distillery of Fowler & Ziegler (Robert Fowler and Frederick K. Ziegler) was the most extensive ever operated in Leitersburg District. It was originally established by John Byer and William E. Doyle in connection with the former's mill on Antietam creek. Fowler & Ziegler purchased the farm, mill, distillery, etc., replaced the old distillery by a substantial stone building equipped with the best appliances known to the business at that time, and supplemented the water power with a twenty horsepower engine. The capacity of the plant was fifty or sixty bushels of grain per day. A considerable quantity of whiskey was stored here during the Civil War, and on one occasion a detachment of Confederate soldiers appropriated sixteen barrels. The operation of the plant was discontinued at the close of the war.

Of the other distilleries mentioned in the foregoing enumeration individual treatment is scarcely possible or necessary. So long as the condition of the trade and the character of the revenue laws were favorable they flourished, and the aggregate business they represented was an economic factor of importance. Every nationality represented in the District—German, Scotch, and English—was also represented in the distilling business; and so were all the churches—Lutheran, Reformed, Protestant Episcopal, Mennonite, Presbyterian. With scarcely an exception the men engaged in it were wealthy, prominent, and influential; but it is simply a statement of fact to assert that the business almost invariably resulted disastrously to their fortunes and their families.

Tanneries, Textile Manufactures, Etc.

A tan-yard is mentioned by Colonel Bouquet as one of the features of the Longmeadows estate in 1765. This casual notice comprises all the information now available regarding it. The tannery operated by John Byer near Leitersburg was situated directly above his mill and comprised about twenty vats. It is probable that this tannery was originally established by Byer, who acquired possession of the property in 1813. It was also operated by Samuel Lantz.

Hemp was once an agricultural product of some importance in the District, and the reduction of the fiber to a condition suitable for the spinning-wheel was equally prominent as a branch of local manufacturing. The raw material was first operated upon by a cone-shaped buhr, resembling the ordinary grist buhr in its mode of action; it was then "scutched" with an oval-shaped, two-edged, wooden hand-knife, and finally "hackled," the instrument used in the latter process resembling a rake fastened to a bench with the teeth turned upward. At this point the spinning-wheel was brought into requisition to convert the product into thread, from which a variety of fabrics could be woven. There were once two hemp-mills in Leitersburg District. That of John Byer was operated in connection with his grist-mill and by the same waterpower. The other was situated on Little Antietam a short distance above the present residence of Levi Hartle.

Another branch of textile manufacture was that pursued by Jacob M. Good on Little Antietam less than half a mile south of Leitersburg near the Smithsburg road and on the farm now owned by Joseph and John B. Barkdoll. This was a carding-mill, operated in a stone building, of which the foundation walls may still be traced. Here the manufacturing process, as in the case of hemp, was preparatory to the spinning-wheel. Good purchased this property from Barnhart B. Light in 1822 and operated it until his death. At an earlier date a carding-mill stood on the farm of Curtis Fogler, near the public road that forms the eastern boundary of the District. The power was derived from the stream that flows through this land.

A gun factory was once located on Little Antietam creek, probably where Freeland W. Anderson now lives. Here Frederick Bell, Jr., built a saw-mill and clover-mill. Nails were once manufactured at a long stone building on the Sprigg estate. About the year 1850 Lewis L. Mentzer conducted the business of coachmaking one mile north of Leitersburg near the Ringgold road.

CHAPTER III.

Leitersburg.

Early History—The Town Plot—The Village in 1830—Business Interests—Secret Societies—Municipal Incorporation—Population.

The site of Leitersburg is embraced in The Resurvey on Well Taught, a tract of thirteen hundred acres granted to George Poe in 1754. In 1762 he sold 362 acres to Jacob Leiter, who died in 1764, having devised it to his youngest sons, Jacob and Peter, by whom it was subsequently divided. As the site of the village was convenient to the Leiter residence it was doubtless reduced to cultivation at an early date and apparently promised no advantages apart from its value for agricultural purposes. There were no indications of future village growth. The nearest public highway was the old Nicholson's Gap road, on the opposite side of the Antietam a mile to the west.

Regarded as a sociological phenomenon, the growth of a village is due to the same causes and subject to the same limitations as that of a city. Its population is attracted by the advantages it offers as a place of residence or business. Great cities are usually situated at the sea, on navigable rivers, or at the convergence of important routes of inland travel; public roads are the corresponding factor in the growth of a country village. In 1802 the Nicholson's Gap road was changed to its present location, and in 1807 the road from Greencastle to the South mountain was opened, intersecting the former a short distance southeast of Antietam creek. In contemporay legal documents the former is also described as "the main road from Hagerstown to the Borough of York in Pennsylvania" and the latter as "the road from Greencastle to Baltimore." In 1811 Andrew Leiter purchased from Jacob Leiter, his father, the land adjacent to the intersection of these roads, and here in 1815 he laid out the town of Leitersburg.

At that date the immediate vicinity of the village was already well improved. Jacob Leiter had died in 1814, but his family still lived at the log house that stands on the farm of Joseph Barkdoll, a short distance west of the village. Near the Antietam creek on the road to Hagerstown stands a stone mansion, built by

George Lantz, who died in 1802; in 1815 this was the residence of his son-in-law, Frederick Ziegler. On the opposite side of the creek were the tannery of Captain John Byer and the mill built by Christian Lantz thirty years before. Christian Russell's mill, now owned by Samuel Strite, had been in operation since 1798, and on the opposite side of the Greencastle road lived the family of George Ziegler, while the residences of William and Joseph Gabby were a short distance farther up the creek. In 1803 Andrew Bachman purchased 103 acres of land along the Smithsburg road adjacent to the Leiter lands and here he was engaged in farming and blacksmithing. The first house on the site of the village was a long, one-story stone building, situated at the northwest corner of the public square where the hotel now stands. There can be little doubt that it was built by Andrew Leiter, who resided there in 1812.

The Town Plot.

The plot of the village shows fifty-three lots, located as follows: Nos. 1 to 14, from the public square to the foot of Water street on the north side; southeast of the square, Nos. 15 to 25 on the north side of the Smithsburg road and Nos. 40 to 50 on the south side; Nos. 33 to 39, southwest from the public square on the west side of the turnpike, and Nos. 51 to 53 on the opposite side; Nos. 26 to 32, northeast of No. 1 on the west side of the turnpike. "The road from Hagerstown towards York," now the turnpike and the main street of the village, is fifty feet wide; the "road from Greencastle towards Baltimore" is sixty feet wide.

The following persons received deeds for lots from Andrew Leiter:

Isaac Clymer, September 15, 1815; No. 28, $90.

Jacob Kessinger, September 16, 1815; Nos. 4, 5, $200; 16, 17, 18, $395; 26, 27, $200.

Lewis Weaver, September 16, 1815; Nos. 7, 29, $174.

Casper Fulk, September 16, 1815; No. 14, $50.

Jacob Houser, September 16, 1815; No. 3, $132.

George Kessinger, August 24, 1816; No. 14, $120.

Adam Lantz, August 24, 1816; No. 6, $100.

Daniel Lowman, August 24, 1816; No. 26, $100.

John Reynolds, August 25, 1816; No. 19, $110.

Joseph Gabby, January 11, 1817; No. 39, $50.
Henry Barnhart, January 11, 1817; Nos. 30, 31, $160.
John Garvin, May 3, 1817; No. 11, $200.
Samuel Myers, October 4, 1817; No. 16, $200.
William Gabby, February 21, 1818; No. 5, $65.
Samuel Houser and John Light, February 21, 1818; No. 2, $200.
George Shiess, April 1, 1818; No. 24, $26.
Henry Shamhart, April 1, 1818; No. 30, $100.
Barnhart B. Light, April 1, 1818; No. 4, $70.
George Kessinger, April 1, 1818; No. 18, $74.
Henry Myer, April 1, 1818; No. 12, $40.
Henry Barnhart, May 13, 1818; No. 1, $900.

Andrew Leiter died in 1818, practically insolvent. He had secured advances from the Hagerstown Bank and The Farmers' and Mechanics' Bank of Greencastle which he was unable to repay, and in the litigation that ensued a number of lots in Leitersburg were sold at sheriff's sale.

The Village in 1830.

In 1830 Christopher Burkhart conducted a hotel at the present residence of David Barnhart, a substantial two-story stone building. Charles A. Fletcher, merchant, and Adam Lantz, laborer, lived on the opposite side of the street, their residences corresponding to the present properties of Joseph Barkdoll and Jacob Creager. Both were one-story log structures. These were the only improvements on the village plot west of the public square; the old Leiter homestead at the extremity of the village was owned by George Poe, blacksmith, and Samuel Leiter, carpenter, lived on the opposite side of the turnpike.

In 1830 Fletcher & Stonebraker's store was located in the substantial brick building at the southeast corner of the square in which Josephus Ground now resides, and John Lahm conducted a hotel at the present residence of Mrs. Charles A. Armour, then a two-story log building. The stone building at the corner of the square in which Andrew Leiter lived in 1812 was still standing and here the Cross Keys Hotel was conducted in 1830. North of this the succession of improvements was as follows: A two-story log building, erected by Daniel Lowman, distiller, and now in-

LEITERSBURG. 105

corporated in the residence of Mrs. Laura K. Ziegler; a two-story log house in which Isaac Clymer, cooper, resided; a one-story log house, the residence of Mrs. Kessinger, a widow; a log house one story and a half high, the present residence of Mrs. John Wolf; a two-story log house, the present residence of Mrs. John Harbaugh; a two-story stone house in which Dr. James Johnson lived and which is now the residence of Jacob B. Mentzer.

On the west side of Water street there was a log building a story and a half high, now the residence of Frank Minor. In 1830 this was the cooper shop in which Amos Dilworth made barrels for Lewis Ziegler's distillery. Mrs. Barbara Leiter, widow of the founder of the town, lived in a one-story log house at the present site of Samuel Minor's; Daniel Lowman, distiller, at the present residence of William Johnson, a one-story log house; Siekman, a weaver, at the present residence of Henry Minor, a log house one story and a half high; Daniel Sheetz, post-fence maker, at a two-story log house at the site of Mrs. Lousia Ziegler's present residence; Frey, a weaver, at Hilary Unclesby's present residence, a one-story stone house; Samuel Light, a shoemaker, at the one-story stone house owned by Freeland W. Anderson.

On the south side of the Smithsburg road John Beckman, blacksmith, and Jacob Martz, wagon-maker, occupied the respective residences of Wilfred L. Flory and Upton Bell, and east of the latter was the Lutheran church. James Slick's residence was occupied by John Beaver, a school teacher. Christian Lantz, tanner, lived to a one-story log house, now the residence of John Lowman; John Fry, a weaver, whose family was remarkable for height, at the present residence of William Shiess. On the opposite side of the street the improvements in 1830 included a log house a story and a half high now incorporated in the residence of Dr. Charles W. Harper; the present residence of Mrs. Catherine Rohrer, a one-story log house; Joseph Leiter's residence, directly opposite the Lutheran church; the residences of Mrs. Ann Leiter and Elizabeth Repp, both log houses a story and a half high; the former was the residence of the late Samuel McDowell and in the latter Daniel J. D. Hicks now lives.

It is evident from the preceding enumeration that the village was composed almost entirely of log houses in 1830. The only brick building was the present residence of Josephus Ground;

there were five stone buildings: the church, Burkhart's hotel, Dr. Johnson's residence, and two small houses on Water street. It is also evident that very few of the houses that constituted the village in 1830 have been removed, although, without exception, they have been enlarged and remodelled until the original structures would no longer be recognized.

BUSINESS INTERESTS.

Among the early hotel-keepers at Leitersburg were Andrew Bachman and Christopher Burkhart, at the present residence of David Barnhart; William Kreps, at the present residence of Josephus Ground; Michael Brunett, and John Lahm, at Mrs. Charles A. Armour's residence. At a later date Samuel Lyday conducted a hotel at the brick building on the Smithsburg road adjacent to the public school grounds. Hotel-keeping was a flourishing business in the days when the Nicholson's Gap road was one of the most important routes of travel in Washington County.

Among the merchants of the village prior to 1840 were Fletcher & Grimes, Fletcher & Stonebraker, Byer & Lantz, and Fletcher & Lantz, who successively conducted business at the southeast corner of the square; Jacob Good and Etnyer & Besore, whose store room occupied the present residence of Charles B. Wolfinger; Jacob Funk, Henry Snider, Joseph Besore, and Kissell & Metz. Besore's store was at the present location of Andrew Hartman's. Between 1840 and 1860 the leading merchants were Fletcher & Good, Etnyer & Martin, Samuel F. Ziegler, George W. Pole, George W. Lahm, and Josephus Ground, who has been engaged in business continuously since 1853. Charles A. Fletcher, Joshua Grimes, Dr. Frederick Byer, Samuel Lantz, Samuel Etnyer, and Charles H. Besore were individual members of the firms mentioned.

The various avocations usually pursued in a country village were early represented. The tailor's craft was pursued by Jonathan Humphreys, Thomas Atkinson, Stephen G. Staley, Alfred Hendricks, and Daniel Lowman; Samuel Light was one of the first shoemakers. Augustus Copeigh (Koppisch) and Andrew Bell were employed as weavers in the vicinity of the village before it was founded and for many years thereafter, and here Frey and Siekman pursued the same occupation at a later date. John

Ziegler was a tinsmith and at the northwest corner of the public square he manufactured copper kettles which enjoyed a high reputation and found purchasers in the adjoining States.

The first village blacksmiths were Andrew Leiter and George Poe, who formed a partnership on the 3d of April, 1816. Their shop was situated on the Greencastle road at the upper end of a triangular field belonging to the Strite's mill property. Poe was subsequently engaged in business individually for some years at the stone blacksmith shop adjacent to the village on the turnpike, and John Beckman was similarly employed at Flory's shop in Leitersburg.

Wagon-making was once an industry of considerable local importance. Samuel Price's shop was located on Water street and Henry Gagle's at Poe's smith shop. In 1844 Upton Bell engaged in this business, which he continued for some years. The wagons he manufactured were especially adapted for heavy hauling and were readily sold.

Samuel Leiter and Joseph Leiter were the carpenters of the village for many years, and either built or rebuilt a majority of the houses. John Shutt was the first undertaker.

The first resident physician was probably Dr. James Johnson, who practiced here from 1827 to 1834. Dr. Frederick Byer located at Leitersburg early in the '30's and continued in practice here until his death. Dr. Thomas B. Duckett was a resident of Leitersburg from 1839 to 1856. Among other local representatives of the medical profession were Doctors Crooks, White, Beard, Good, and Harper.

A business directory at the present time would include the following names: Josephus Ground, Andrew Hartman, dealers in general merchandise; Isaac G. Leiter, David Barnhart, William L. Shiess, carpenters and contractors; Wilfred L. Flory, blacksmith; Charles C. Ziegler, cable-wire fence contractor; J. H. Wishard, M. D.; Charles E. Poe, V. S.; D. J. D. Hicks, secretary of the Planters' Mutual Insurance Company; Jacob M. Stouffer, postmaster; Frank D. Bell, justice of the peace; Virgil H. Miller, William Anderson, confectioners; A. H. Bowers, dealer in country produce; John C. Strite, miller; Michael Niuffer, shoemaker; Samuel Minor, Hilary Unclesby, masons; John Shatzer, hotelkeeper.

INSURANCE COMPANY.

The Planters' Mutual Insurance Company of Washington County was incorporated by the Maryland Legislature in March, 1846. The charter of the company designated Joseph Gabby, Jacob E. Bell, Christian Strite, David M. Good, Joseph Leiter, and George L. Ziegler as its first directors, and on the 19th of March, 1846, they organized by electing David M. Good as president. At this meeting the president appointed Joseph Leiter, Abraham Strite, Christian Strite, Jacob E. Bell, and George L. Ziegler as assistant surveyors, and the work of soliciting insurance seems to have been at once begun. The first policy was issued on the 22d of September, 1847, in favor of Lewis Ziegler.

The following is a list of presidents of the Company with dates of their election to office: David M. Good, March 19, 1846; Joseph Leiter, March 20, 1847; William B. McAtee, August 2, 1862; Jacob E. Bell, September 9, 1865; David M. Deitrich, September 20, 1873; David Strite, September 20, 1884; David Hoover, February 15, 1896.

Christian Strite was elected secretary, March 20, 1847; Samuel Etnyer, September, 1847; Josephus Ground, November 3, 1855; James A. Hays, July 24, 1886; Lewis J. Ground, September 21, 1889; D. J. D. Hicks, the present incumbent, April 30, 1891.

Jacob E. Bell was elected treasurer, March 20, 1847; David M. Good, June 16, 1849; Samuel F. Ziegler, September 20, 1851; Jacob A. Metz, September 18, 1852; Josephus Ground, September 9, 1854; George W. Pole, November 3, 1855; Josephus Ground, May, 1886; J. Freeland Leiter, July, 1886; Samuel Strite, August, 1891.

The property insured by this company is located principally in the counties of Washington, Frederick, Montgomery, Carroll, Caroline, Dorchester, and Somerset, in Maryland; Franklin, in Pennsylvania, and Loudoun, in Virginia. The assets of the company consist almost entirely of premium notes, representing from ten to fifty per cent. of the amount insured, the rates varying with the nature of the risk. The cost of insurance is from two to five per cent. of the premium note, depending on the length of time the policy is in force. During the fifty years the company has been engaged in business it has levied fifteen assessments, aggregating forty-five per cent. of its premium notes. The last annual

LUTHERAN CHURCH, LEITERSBURG.

statement of the company (December 31, 1897) shows aggregate risks in force, $934,139.90; aggregate assets, $153,637.08, of which $152,109.69 consisted of premium notes; aggregate disbursements for the year 1897, $9,999.87, of which $8,257.70 represented the amount of losses paid.

Secret Societies.

Howard Lodge, Independent Order of Good Templars, was organized on the 28th of June, 1846, with the following officers: Edward Smith, W. C. T.; James A. Hays, W. S.; Maggie P. Waggoner, W. I. G.; Alice M. Staley, W. V. T.; Daniel Wolfinger, W. T.; James H. Ziegler, W. O. G. The organization disbanded about the year 1873.

A lodge of the Independent Order of American Mechanics was instituted in 1871 with the following officers: James A. Hays, W. S. M.; Henry Schriver, W. M.; John W. Nigh, J. M.; David Summer, R. S.; H. T. Creps, S.; Upton Clopper, T.; Edward Smith, C.

Golden Rod Council, No. 42, Junior Order United American Mechanics, was chartered December 22, 1891, with the following officers: Charles C. Ziegler, P. C.; D. J. D. Hicks, C.; Jacob D. Wolfinger, R. S.; David Barnhart, F. S.; Samuel Middlekauff, T. In 1897 the Council erected a hall at a cost of $2,000. It is a two-story frame building, of which the first floor constitutes an auditorium in which public meetings of a general character are held; the council rooms occupy the second floor. Samuel Middlekauff, Charles C. Ziegler, and Jacob M. Stouffer composed the building committee. It was dedicated with appropriate ceremonies on the 12th of September, 1897.

Minneola Tribe, No. 114, Independent Order of Red Men, was instituted April 10, 1895, with the following officers; Joseph S. Barkdoll, P.; D. J. D. Hicks, S.; Samuel Middlekauff, S. S.; B. F. Baker, J. S.; Daniel T. Johnson, C. of R.; Virgil H. Miller, C. of W.; Harvey J. Hartle, K. of W.; Daniel T. Hartle, G. of W.; Claggett A. Hartle, G. of F.

Municipal Incorporation.

Leitersburg was incorporated by act of the Legislature, February 25, 1853, with the following boundaries:

Commencing at a poplar tree on the road leading from Leitersburg to Smithsburg near a stable belonging to Jeremiah Slick, thence running with a straight line to a stable near the house now occupied by Daniel Lowman, thence with a straight line to a spring on or near a lot belonging to Nathan McDowell on the road leading from Leitersburg to Greencastle, thence with a straight line to a blacksmith shop now occupied by G. W. Lantz belonging to George Poe, thence with a straight line to the beginning.

The act of incorporation provided for the annual election of a burgess, assistant burgess, and three commissioners, whose functions were minutely defined. The first election occurred on the first Monday in April, 1853. The local government was duly organized, and under its administration the streets were improved, the sidewalks were curbed and paved, and other measures of benefit to the community inaugurated. But after several annual elections had been held the town government dissolved and no effort has since been made to reestablish it.

POPULATION.

The late George W. Ziegler of Greencastle informed the writer that in 1829 he made an enumeration of the inhabitants of Leitersburg and found a population of 219. In 1850 it was 298; in 1870, 335; in 1880, 308. No statistics are given in the census of 1890.

CHAPTER IV.

CHURCHES.

ANTIETAM LUTHERAN CHURCH—JACOBS LUTHERAN CHURCH—ST. PAUL'S LUTHERAN CHURCH, LEITERSBURG—ST. JAMES' REFORMED CHURCH, LEITERSBURG — MILLER'S MENNONITE CHURCH — LONGMEADOWS GERMAN BAPTIST CHURCH—REFORMED MENNONITE—RIVER BRETHREN—UNITED BRETHREN CHURCH, LEITERSBURG — METHODIST EPISCOPAL CHURCH, LEITERSBURG.

ONE of the oldest churches in Washington County was situated within the original limits of Leitersburg District. There is conclusive evidence of its existence at an earlier date than that of any other place of worship in the county, with the possible exception of St. Paul's near Clearspring and the Protestant Episcopal chapel near Chapel Woods school in Funkstown District, not far from the College of St. James. This evidence occurs in the will of Robert Downing, executed on the 1st of November, 1754. The clause referring to this church reads as follows:

I give and bequeath to my beloved daughter, Esther Downing, all that tract or parcel of land, part of the second resurvey on Downing's Lot, beginning at the most easternmost corner of the first resurvey on Downing's Lot and running thence south forty-five degrees west six perches across the second resurvey and all the land on the most southernmost side of the before mentioned line, containing by estimation 113 acres of land, excepting ten acres to be laid out for and convenient to the meeting house, provided the people that resort to the said meeting house pay for it.

In 1786 the Rev. John George Young, pastor of St. John's Lutheran Church, Hagerstown, wrote the following account of this church:

1756.—About thirteen families of our church united, purchased ten acres of land, and built a sort of church, as their circumstances allowed, about four miles from Hagerstown on the Antietam creek. They were served first for several years by Pastor Haushihl from Frederick and then for a short time by Pastor Schwerdtfeger; finally, after I received a call from Hagerstown I was also called there and served them every four weeks until, on account of other pressing duties, I was compelled last year to relinquish this part of the field. They consist now of from fifty-five to sixty families, many of whom with respect to their spiritual welfare were thoroughly ruined by the late war, so that little improvement is to be expected. From this congregation four others have originated, viz., Hagerstown, Funkstown, Manorland, and Conococheague.

On the 9th of June, 1787, Martin Ridenour and John Beard "by and with the consent of the Lutheran congregation belonging to Antietam church, for and in consideration of the sum of £42," executed a deed to William Shanafield for nine and one-half acres of land, part of a tract of ten acres called God Save the Church, subject to the following reservations:

> One-half acre thereof, whereon there stands a church and church yard, two perches added on the west side and two perches on the south side of said church yard, together with the church yard, will contain one-half acre of land, the same to be exempted forever; the wagon road from Rohrer's mill to said Shanafield's house through said ten acres of land is to be kept open, free, and clear, that there may be a clear passage to said church and the yard forever.

Rohrer's mill was built before the Revolution; it is situated on Antietam creek four miles from Hagerstown and half a mile from the turnpike leading from that city to Smithsburg. The present owner is Joseph Trovinger. In the immediate vicinity Shanafield acquired a tract of three hundred acres, to which he gave the name of Rock Hall. It is now embraced principally in the farm of Daniel Doub, and the house referred to in the deed of 1787 was probably the present farm house. The present public road follows the north bank of the creek; in 1787 the road from the mill to the farm house must have pursued a different course. The church site and burial ground are embraced in Mr. Doub's farm, about midway between the farm house and the mill and at a distance of about two hundred yards from the creek, to which there is a gradual slope. The opposite bank is steep, rugged, and picturesque.

The tract of ten acres referred to in Robert Downing's will is readily identified with that of Beard and Ridenour's deed, although no deed for the church land has been discovered. Esther Downing died without issue, and in compliance with the terms of her father's will her part of his estate reverted to her brothers and sisters. Her oldest sister, Elizabeth, married Robert Blackburn, of Frederick County, Va., and in 1767 they executed a deed to John Rohrer for twenty-eight acres of land in the immediate vicinity of the church, part of the 113 acres bequeathed to Esther

Downing. In 1786 Joseph Downing executed a deed to William Shanafield for twenty-six acres adjacent to the church land, also part of Esther Downing's bequest. And since this 113 acres adjoined on two sides the tract of ten acres referred to in Beard and Ridenour's deed of 1787, the conclusion is irresistible that it was identical with the reservation of ten acres for which Robert Downing provided in his will in 1754.

It may be observed that the will refers to the meeting house as already built, while the Rev. John George Young says it was built in 1756. But the will was a contemporary document while Mr. Young obtained his information from hearsay thirty years later; therefore the evidence of the former must be accepted. Downing secured the warrant for his second resurvey, March 24, 1753; it was renewed in 1754, and the patent was issued in 1755 under date of April 4th. No reference to the meeting house occurs in this document.

From Mr. Young's account it is evident that this was the mother Lutheran church of Washington County. The information that he gives regarding its numerical strength is also valuable while the references to Haushihl and Schwerdtfeger show that it was originally under the same pastoral jurisdiction as the church at Frederick, Md. Rev. Bernard Michael Haushihl was born in Wurtemberg in 1727, obtained his education at the University of Strassburg, and was ordained at Rotterdam. He arrived at Annapolis, Md., in 1752, and resided at Frederick until 1758. From 1770 to 1783 he was pastor of the Dutch Lutheran Church in New York City. He was an ardent Royalist and after the Revolution moved to Halifax, Nova Scotia, where he died in 1797. He was an eloquent and learned man. If, as Mr. Young states, he was the first pastor of Antietam church, it could not have been organized prior to 1753.

Rev. John William Samuel Schwerdtfeger was pastor at Frederick from 1763 to 1768, when he returned temporarily to Europe, leaving Rev. J. G. Hartwick in charge of his congregations. The following entry occurs in the journal of the Rev. Henry Melchoir Muhlenburg concerning the meeting of the Ministerium of Pennsylvania in 1769:

The congregations which up to the present have entered a written petition for the reception of Mr. Wildbahn into the Ministerium are:

I. In Pennsylvania: Jacobs Church, Codorus township, St. John's Church, Germany township, York County.

II. In Maryland: On Silver run, on the Great Pipe creek, on Thomas creek, on Oliver's creek, Frederick County; in Conococheague: on Antietam creek; in Sharpsburg on the Potomac.

III. In Virginia: Shepherdstown; Winchestertown.

Rev. Charles Frederick Wildbahn resided at the time near Littlestown, Pa.; the wide extent of territory embraced in his pastoral jurisdiction is shown by the preceding list of congregations. In 1770 he moved to MacAllistertown (now Hanover, Pa.), and his continuance as pastor of congregations so far from his home was opposed at the next meeting of the Ministerium, when one of the questions considered was: "The separation of the Conococheague congregations from MacAllistertown." The following entry occurs in the minutes for 1772: "A delegate from vacant congregations in a region situated between the boundaries of Pennsylvania and Virginia in Maryland and called by the Indian name Conococheague, which Senior Kurtz visited now and then and administered therein the means of grace, and which is also said to be very populous and surrounded by all sorts of sectarian religious parties, laid before the Ministerium a petition for an able teacher and pastor and said to me privately that they desired the older Mr. Kurtz." The younger Kurtz was accordingly sent thither as shown by the following entry in the minutes for 1773: "A petition from four congregations in the Conococheague district in Maryland connected with the Ministerium, in which they petition for Frederick Muhlenberg as their pastor and preacher, because Mr. Kurtz, Jr., who had been appointed for the place at the preceding synodical meeting, could not get along well." Three of these congregations were undoubtedly Antietam, Sharpsburg, and Hagerstown; the fourth was probably Jerusalem (Funkstown). Rev. Frederick Augustus Muhlenberg accordingly acted as supply for a short time. He was subsequently a member of the Continental Congress, chairman of the first constitutional convention of Pennsylvania, and Speaker of the first House of Representatives of the United States.

In the same year (1773) Rev. John George Young located at Hagerstown, where he was pastor of St. John's and other churches in the county until his death, April 26, 1793. His pastorate at Antietam ceased in 1785. In 1787 the congregation erected a new church at the present site of Beard's, or St. Peter's, now in Chewsville District, but formerly in Leitersburg.*

The original reservation of half an acre at the old church site was gradually encroached upon. Some years ago many of the grave-stones were pulled out and utilized in the construction of a culvert. A few were spared for a time, however, and in 1887, a hundred years after the sale to Shanafield, the burial ground was still thirty-five feet long and twelve feet wide, with several tombstones in a horizontal position, one inscribed with the year 1763 as the date of death. Within the next ten years, however, all this was removed, and on the occasion of the author's visit in the autumn of 1897 only the stump of a wild cherry tree remained to mark the place. It is disgraceful to a civilized community that a spot hallowed by Christian worship and Christian burial, the oldest church site in the valley of the Antietam, the last resting-place of many of the pioneers and doubtless of some who rendered loyal service in the French and Indian War and in the Revolution, should be thus desecrated.

JACOBS LUTHERAN CHURCH.

Of all the institutions of Leitersburg District, the oldest is Jacobs Church. It was founded more than a score of years before the village of Leitersburg and nearly a decade before the more pretentious borough of Waynesboro. In the consideration of its history we revert to the period when many of the first permanent settlers were still living—the men and women who had successfully contested with wild nature and the wilder savage for their farms and homes in the valley of the upper Antietam.

The Lutheran congregation that worshiped on the banks of the Antietam in 1754 doubtless numbered among its membership some of the families afterward embraced in the constituency of Jacobs Church. Others were members of St. John's at Hagerstown, organized prior to 1769; of the church at Grindstone Hill in Franklin County, Pa., which was in existence as early as 1765; or of Zion Lutheran Church at Greencastle, also one of the oldest in Franklin County. The date at which Jacobs Church was organized can not be satisfactorily determined, but there is reason

---

* For the citations from the protocol of the Ministerium of Pennsylvania contained in this sketch the author is indebted to Rev. Henry E. Jacobs, D. D.

to believe that this occurred in 1791. The grounds for this conclusion are as follows:

The records of St. John's Lutheran Church at Hagerstown show that several Lutheran families from this locality were members there from 1770 to 1780. Peter and Anthony Bell were among those whose names occur in this connection; and as they lived within a mile of Jacobs church it is not probable that they would have journeyed so far if an organization had existed in the immediate vicinity at the time. In 1786 Rev. John George Young of Hagerstown prepared a brief historical sketch of the churches of his charge in which, referring to Beard's, he says: "From this congregation four others have originated, viz., Hagerstown, Funkstown, Manorland, and Conococheague." Mr. Young's pastorate embraced the churches referred to, as well as others in Frederick County. If Jacobs Church had been organized at this time it is more than probable that it would have been part of his charge, or that he would in any case have mentioned it; hence its omission affords strong presumptive evidence that it had no existence in 1786. Furthermore, the present church grounds were not acquired from the State until 1787, and it is extremely improbable that a church building would have been erected here before that date.

Affirmatively, it may be positively stated that the church was organized in the year 1791 or prior thereto, as the protocol of the Ministerium of Pennsylvania shows that the Rev. Guenther Wingardt was pastor from 1791 to 1795. While this evidence is conclusive, it leaves to doubt and conjecture much that would be most interesting regarding the circumstances under which the organization was effected. Wingardt was succeeded by Rev. John Ruthrauff in 1795, and with this date adequate local records begin. The earliest document of this description is a list of subscriptions for his support. It reads as follows:

Ein Verzeichniss von denjenigen Gemeinde Glieder und anderen guten Freunden der Gemeinde an der so genannten Freidens Kirche welche bewilligt sind zum Unterhalt des Predigers und zur fernern Fortsetzung des Gottes Dienstes an den Herrn Johannes Ruthrauff als unser Prediger das ihrige mit beizutragen, die werden deswegen ersucht das sie sich in den Pfrunde Zettel ihre Namen sich unterschreiben zu lassen. Der Anfang dieses Jahres wird wohl sein als den 5te Julius, 1795.

CHURCHES.

Die Namen der Gemeinde Glieder.	Was ein Jeder Geben will.	
	Pf.	Sch.
Alt Christian Lantz, Altester,	1 2	6
Anthony Bell, Altester,	2 0	0
Johannes Hafner, Vorsteher,	0 15	0
Heinrich Jacob, Vorsteher,	0 10	0

This may be translated as follows:

A list of those church members and other friends of the congregation known as Friedens Church who are willing to contribute to the support of the pastor and the further continuance of divine worship with Rev. John Ruthrauff as our pastor, and who may be solicited to enter their names for this purpose in the subscription list of the church. The current year will begin with the 5th of July, 1795.

Names of Church Members.	What Each One Will Give.		
	£	s.	d.
Christian Lantz, Sr., elder,	1	2	6
Anthony Bell, elder,	2	0	0
John Hafner, deacon,	0	15	0
Henry Jacobs, deacon,	0	10	0

In addition to the officers of the church, subscriptions were also made by the following persons:

Christopher Burkhart,
Jacob Ritter,
Adam Lyday,
Christian Pfeiffer,
Carl Goll,
George Baker,
Christopher Burkhart, Jr.,
Jacob Huber,
George Augenstein,
Ludwig Emerick,
George Baker, Jr.,
John Bell,
David Scholl,
Johannes Dornwart,
Jacob May,
Herman Stolz,
David Besore,
Jacob Busch.

David Ritter,
Martin Jacobs,
Philip Ripple,
Felix Wagner,
Jacob Leiter, Sr.,
George Lantz,
George Burkhart,
Michael Summers,
John Wesenman,
Andrew Bell,
Jacob Ritter,
——— Fruhlig,
Christian Lantz, Jr.,
Frederick Nicodemus,
Michael Altig,
Henry Jirb,
Henry Miller,
John Mentzer.

In a similar subscription list for 1796 the following additional names appear: Alexander Duncan, John Dorbart, Jacob Grove,

Davis Sittro, Frederick Mero, William Ebrad, George Leiter, Sr., Simon Fogler, Frederick Wagner, Michael Wolfinger, and Matthias Summers.

Within a few years after the Rev. John Ruthrauff became pastor he proposed a constitution for the church, which was duly adopted and signed by the officers and members on the 23d of September, 1798. This document is entitled "Kirchen Artikel für die Evangelische Lutherische Gemeinde liegend an der Linie von Maryland und Pennsylvania—die Friedens Kirche genannt" —"Constitution for the Evangelical Lutheran Congregation situated at the Maryland and Pennsylvania line, called Peace Church." It defines in detail the duties of pastor, council, and members. The church council at that time was composed of Jacob Rider, Anthony Bell, Philip Ripple, David Goll, and John Bell.

The membership at this time was widely scattered. Four other Lutheran churches have since been organized upon the original territory of Jacobs Church, located, respectively, at Waynesboro, Leitersburg, Quincy, and Rouzerville. The formation of the two first named practically reduced the congregation to its present limits. Its numerical strength has varied widely. In 1796 the number of communicants was 33, but in 1798 105 persons attached their names to the constitution as members and officers. The formation of the Waynesboro congregation in 1818 undoubtedly deprived the mother church of many members, but defective records at this period render it impossible to estimate the loss. In 1826, after the organization of the Leitersburg church, there were still 76 communicants at Jacobs. In 1830 the number was 93; in 1835, 67; May 26, 1839, 65; April 30, 1843, 87; May 11, 1845, 88; June 4, 1848, 97; May 19, 1850, 102; May 13, 1855, 85; May 19, 1860, 70; November 21, 1869, 64; April 27, 1879, 65; September 20, 1885, 61; October 31, 1897, 69. The following note is appended to a communion record in 1855: "This congregation has lost a considerable number of members by removal." This remark would apply to the church at almost any period in its history. Many families have removed from its bounds at various times and located in neighboring towns or in the West, where they have in more than one locality been active in establishing or sustaining other Lutheran churches.

CHURCHES.

The regulations governing the baptism of children at the organization of the church are a part of the first constitution; the earliest baptismal entries, which are also the earliest records extant, are herewith given:

> Frederick Bell et uxor Rosina; sohn, Johannes; gebohren den 29 Juni; getauft den 6te November, 1791. Taufzeichen, Johannes Bell et Margaretha Bell.
> Martin Lauman et uxor Regina Elizabeth; tochter, Eva; gebohren 1791 den 20te October; getauft den 6te November, 1791. Taufzeichen, Heinrich Jacob, Elizabeth ———.
> Andreas Leiter et uxor Barbara; tochter, Susanna Catharina; gebohren 1791 den 3te Juli; getauft den 6te November, 1791. Taufzeichen, Jacob Leiter et uxor Juliana.
> 1797, den 24te Februar ist Heinrich Jacob und seiner frau Anna Maria ein Sohnlein zur Welt gebohren, n. Johan Heinrich. Taufziechen sind die Eltern. Getauft, 1797, den 2te April.

Throughout this old register German surnames are invariably given. Among those that occur most frequently are Johannes, Georg, Andreas, Anton, Heinrich, Friedrich, Mattheus, Leonhardt, Ludwig, Dorothea, Margaretha, Regina, Maria, Catharina, Elizabeth. German was also the language of public worship throughout the ministry of Rev. John Ruthrauff.

The site of the church and the burial ground adjacent are embraced in a tract of land called Martin's Good Hope. Martin Jacobs secured a warrant for the survey of this tract on the 21st of August, 1787; the survey was made on the 1st of April, 1788, and a patent was issued in his favor, September 21, 1790. The area of the tract was eighteen acres. The church land was deeded by Martin Jacobs to Christian Lantz "for the use of the German Lutheran congregation and their successors," November 18, 1799, at the nominal consideration of five shillings "and in consideration of divers other good causes him the said Martin Jacob thereunto moving." It contained three-fourths of an acre and thirty-four perches of land "together with the church thereon and other the appurtenances thereunto belonging."

Here many of the settlers of Leitersburg District and the adjacent township in Pennsylvania are buried. But unfortunately no intelligible memorials mark the graves of many of them. The tombstones are limestone specimens, evidently selected with some regard for smoothness of surface and regularity of form, but destitute of information regarding those whose last resting places they are intended to perpetuate. It is probable that George Jacobs, a son of the donor of the land, was one of the first persons interred here, as the date of his death, November 16, 1790, is the earliest inscription of this character that has been discovered.

From the deed for the church land it is evident that the church building had been erected thereon at that time; how much earlier it may have been built is matter of conjecture, but it is extremely improbable that this occurred prior to 1787, when the land was acquired by Martin Jacobs. For this was a substantial and somewhat pretentious building, one that the projectors would scarcely have erected upon land that might possibly have become vested in an owner indifferent or unfriendly to their interests. Regarding the cost of this building or the persons responsibly connected with the enterprise no particulars have been preserved. There is, however, in one of the old church records a memorandum of subscriptions for the "Kirch Decken" (church roof), for which some made contributions in money and others in labor. The same plan doubtless prevailed in the erection of the building. Trees were felled in the surrounding forest, and from their trunks the logs were hewn that formed its walls. "The raising" was no doubt a grand affair, distinguished by the conviviality usual on such occasions, and participated in by the entire membership and their friends. The last great event was the day of dedication, when pastor and people set apart the house they had built as a place of public worship, and such it continued to be for about fifty years.

This building occupied the site of the present brick structure. In form it was nearly square, each side being about twenty-five feet in length. The entrance was at the middle of the south side, and was reached by steps of large, flat stones. There were two doors, as in the main entrance to the present building, but they were constructed with battens instead of panels. Prior to 1825 the church was weather-boarded and painted a nondescript color intermediate between white and yellow.

To an observer of the present generation perhaps the most striking feature of the interior would have been the pulpit. This was an octagonal enclosure at the middle of the north side, and directly opposite the entrance. It was supported on a pillar at a height of six feet from the level of the floor, and was reached by a narrow stairway at the left or east side. Its furniture consisted of a shelf in front, supported by a cornice, on which the Bible rested, and an uncushioned seat placed against the wall. After the preacher had ascended the stairway and entered the sacred enclosure that was peculiarly and exclusively his own he had space to stand comfortably or to sit with such comfort as he could. An assisting clergyman was obliged to take his place among the laity, as the pulpit was too small to accommodate two.

The aisle extended from the entrance to the pulpit. The men occupied the east or right side, the women the west or left side. The benches were securely fastened to the floor; they consisted of a horizontal seat and a back-rest six inches wide, supported at each end and in the middle. A gallery, supported by columns, extended across the south and west sides over the door and the pews occupied by the women. Here the seats were arranged in three tiers, with a balustrade in front of the lower tier. At the south side of the church a stairway ascended from the door to the corner of the gallery. In front of the pulpit there was an open space, in which were placed a substantial panelled table used on communion occasions and a plain bench at which candidates for confirmation knelt. Here, too, conspicuously in front of the pulpit, the *vorsanger* or precentor sat, with a little bench before him on which he placed his books. Back of the precentor and on his right were seated the church council, some of whom could always observe anything that occurred without turning around. This was the post of honor as well as duty. Immediately after installation the elders and deacons took their places here, and here they sat as long as their official incumbency continued. One important duty of the *vorsteher* was to pass the *Klingenseckel* (tinkling pocket), a velvet bag with pendant tassel and bell, supported by an iron hoop at the end of a long pole. The bell was doubtless intended to arouse somnolent members to a sense of their financial duties. Originally the furniture of the church comprised neither lamp nor stove, and there was no artificial provision for either light or heat. About the year 1825 a large ten-plate stove was placed in the center of the church, and as there was no chimney, the pipe passed out through the roof.

Such was the building in which the fathers of this church worshiped. It survived, in all probability, all who were prominently identified with its erection. But the time at length arrived when its usefulness was terminated. In 1841 it was removed; the logs were hauled to Leitersburg and used in the construction of two houses, now owned, respectively, by Jacob Stouffer and Mrs. Sarah Tritle. That of Mrs. Tritle was formerly the United Brethren parsonage.

The following account of the building of the present church was contributed by Rev. John P. Cline of Smithsburg, Md., to the *Lutheran Observer* of December 31, 1841: "On the 10th of September last the corner-stone of a new church was laid within Rev. F. W. Conrad's charge, in Washington County, Md.; and on Sunday, the 5th inst., it was already consecrated to the service of the Triune God. This was truly expeditious work. At the laying of the corner-stone the Rev. Messrs. Bomberger and Hoffmeyer of the German Reformed Church and Sahm, E. Keller, Conrad, and the writer of the Lutheran church were present. At the dedication Brothers Startzman, Conrad, and the subscriber officiated. The new church occupies the site of the old one. The old one was named 'Friedens Kirche' (commonly known as Jacobs church), and the new one was named 'Jacobs church.' It can not be said of this house as was said of the second Temple; for the second is superior to the first. It is built of brick; is neat and comfortable. It is exclusively Lutheran." Supplementary to this it may be stated that the contractor for its erection was Joseph Leiter, of Leitersburg, who accepted the old church in partial payment for his work.

In 1854 the church building was enlarged to its present dimensions by an addition about sixteen feet in length at the western end. Other repairs were also made at this time, and the remodeled edifice was first occupied for divine service on the 10th of December, 1854. This was a communion occasion, in which the pastor, Rev. John Heck, was assisted by Rev. H. F. Early. Extensive repairs were again made in 1881, after which the church was formally reopened on the 1st of January, 1882. The clergy present were Reverends P. Bergstresser, L. J. Bell, X. J. Richardson, and V. Miller, who delivered a sermon appropriate to the occasion. Ten years later the interior was again remodeled, the principal improvement being the present pews.

The opening service occurred on the 1st of May, 1892, when the pastor, Rev. H. S. Cook, and Rev. E. H. Delk were the officiating clergymen.

The fence surrounding the church grounds has been repaired and rebuilt at various times. In 1897 Malinda B. Jacobs presented to the congregation the handsome and substantial iron gates formerly used at one of the entrances to Green Hill cemetery near Waynesboro. The post-and-rail fence in front of the church was forthwith removed and replaced with the present one, adding greatly to the appearance and convenience of the church grounds.

The following is a list of pastors of Jacobs Church since 1791:

1791-95, Guenther Wingardt.
1795-1835, John Ruthrauff.
1835-37, Jeremiah Harpel.
1837-39, Jacob Martin.
1840, Peter Sahm, D. D.
1841-44, F. W. Conrad, D. D.
1845-56, John Heck.
1857-62, J. F. Campbell.
1863, Edwin Dorsey.
1864-71, Alfred Buhrman.
1871-75, C. L. Keedy.
1876-87, P. Bergstresser, D. D.
1888, H. S. Cook.

Wingardt resided at Taneytown, Md., and was pastor of the following churches: Taneytown, Jacobs, Winter's, Thomas Creek, Upper Bermudian, Zion, and Flohr's. The charge to which Ruthrauff was assigned in 1795 was composed of Greencastle, Jacobs, Beard's, Mayfield (?), and Mercersburg, but its limits varied at different times during his long pastorate. He resided at Greencastle, and Jacobs was part of the Greencastle charge until 1841, when the Waynesboro charge was formed; the original constituent churches were Waynesboro, Jacobs, Quincy, and Funkstown. For some years past the Waynesboro and Jacobs Churches have constituted a charge.

Of the several auxiliary organizations connected with Jacobs Church the oldest is the Sunday school. A German school was organized about the year 1830, but it was not a success. An English Sunday school was also conducted for a time at the school house on the church grounds with John Beaver as superintendent. When Harpel became pastor an effort was again made to organize, and from that time the school has been conducted every year to the present time. The first election of which there is any record occurred on the 6th of May, 1837, resulting in the choice of John Jacobs and Frederick Bell as superintendents,

John Ross, secretary, and Henry Jacobs, treasurer. The organization was known as "The Peace Church Sunday School Union," and the school was opened in the spring and closed in the fall. In 1837 there were eighteen male teachers and six female teachers, thirty-three male scholars and seventeen female scholars. The following is a partial list of subsequent superintendents: John Jacobs, John Uhler, Henry Jacobs, Daniel Bell, John Walter, Henry Oaks, Joseph S. Mentzer, Walter S. Mentzer, John Harbaugh, Joseph M. Bell, and Samuel Cook. The present constitution of the school was adopted on the 1st of April, 1866.

The following entry occurs in the minutes of the school under date of July 17, 1842:

> *Resolved*, That we hold a Sabbath school celebration at Jacobs church, Saturday, 6th August, 1842, and that the Rev. Mr. Bomberger of the Reformed Church, Rev. Mr. Kline of the Lutheran Church, and Rev. Mr. Conrad of this church be invited to attend; and that the Leitersburg, Waynesboro, and the Besore [Salem] Church Sabbath schools be invited to attend.

A committee of arrangements was also appointed, and the "celebration" was doubtless a success. These occasions differed somewhat from the modern picnic. The public addresses and demonstrations were patriotic in character as well as religious, but the social feature of the occasion predominated in the "celebration" no less than in its modern successor.

The Friedens Church Education and Missionary Society was in existence in 1830. Henry Jacobs was treasurer, and his receipts for the year amounted to $28.33.

The Young People's Society of Christian Endeavor was organized in January, 1892, with seventeen active members and two associate members. The first officers were Ernest E. Bell, president; C. L. Walter, vice-president; Ida M. Bell, recording secretary; Meta Walter, corresponding secretary; Otho Kahl, treasurer.

The Woman's Home and Foreign Missionary Society was organized on the 9th of May, 1893, with the following officers: President, Mrs. Joseph M. Bell; vice-president, Mrs. Samuel Cook; recording secretary, Mary Cook; corresponding secretary, Meta Walter; treasurer, Mrs. C. L. Walter.

St. Paul's Lutheran Church, Leitersburg.

The oldest original document relating to the history of this church bears the following title: "Unser Grundsatze beim Ecksteinlegen der Evangelisch Lutherischen Kirche in Leitersburg." As German would probably be unintelligible to readers of this book, an English translation is herewith given:

Declaration of our Principles at the laying of the Corner-stone of the Evangelical Lutheran Church in Leitersburg:

In the name of the Triune God, Amen.

Since the members of the Evangelical Lutheran Church in and about Leitersburg, in Washington County and State of Maryland, have no house of their own for the special purpose of divine worship and one is necessary for the maintenance of religion, for convenience in hearing the sacred Word, for the administration of the holy sacraments, and for our own salvation as well as that of our children and children's children; and since the congregation in the past year has greatly increased and has now decided to build one, it is proposed to proclaim to the world with what intention, for what purpose, and on what principles of Christianity this house is built.

Therefore, we hereby declare for the information of the present and future generations that here this day, the 6th of August in the year of our Lord and Saviour Jesus Christ 1826 and of the independence of the United States of North America the fiftieth, under the administration of President John Quincy Adams and John C. Calhoun, Vice-President, and of Joseph Kent, Governor of Maryland, we lay the corner-stone of a German Evangelical Lutheran church; and that if God prospers the work under our hands and the building is finished, it shall be dedicated to the Triune God, Father, Son, and Holy Ghost, and so remain forever, and shall be called

St. Paul's Church.

That it shall be and remain an Evangelical Lutheran church, wherein the pure and unalloyed Gospel shall be preached and the holy sacraments administered according to the teachings of Christ and the Augsburg Confession, the contents of which we have in our catechism, which we now, in conclusion, place in the corner-stone, that in time to come it may be seen what was the confession of our faith. Should men arise after us who forget their Saviour, despise God's word and sacraments, and will not endure sound doctrine, we take Heaven and Earth as witnesses that we are not to blame but are pure from the blood of all men. We take Heaven and Earth as witnesses of our attachment to Evangelical Christianity and that its extension is our most ardent desire; that it is our wish that the doctrine of Christ's atonement may be proclaimed to destitute souls here in this place; that we expect our children and children's children never to forsake their church, but to be true to it; that it is our wish that here old and young may be edified, animated, encouraged, and prepared for eternity. With such desires and with such prospects we may confidently hope and with Jacob say: This stone which we here set up as a memorial shall be God's house, a place where He manifests His presence.

Done at Leitersburg on the 6th day of August in the year of our Lord and Saviour Jesus Christ 1826 and in the fiftieth year of the independence of the United States of North America, and signed by the ministers present and the members of the building committee:

Ministers' Names.	Names of Building Committee.
John Ruthrauff,	Christopher Burkhart,
Frederick Ruthrauff,	Frederick Bell,
Henry Kroh,	Frederick Ziegler,
Jacob Medtart.	Lewis Ziegler,
	Joshua Grimes.
	Jacob Tanner, Contractor.

This document further states that the first sermon was preached by Rev. John Ruthrauff from Jude 21, 22; the second sermon, by Rev. Frederick Ruthrauff, from Eph. ii. 19-22; the third sermon, in English, by Rev. Jacob Medtart, from Isa. xxviii. 16; and the fourth sermon, by Rev. Henry Kroh, from I. Cor. x. 31-33.

It thus appears that there was no church edifice at Leitersburg for more than a decade after the village was founded. The nearest places of worship were Beard's and Jacobs churches, each several miles distant and in opposite directions. The organization of a congregation doubtless preceded the erection of a church building. This is evident from a clause in the document just quoted, "since the congregation in the past year has greatly increased." At this time Rev. Benjamin Kurtz was the Lutheran pastor at Hagerstown, and his charge also embraced Beard's, with which many of the Lutheran families of Leitersburg District were connected; but during his absence in Europe (1825-27) Revs. John Ruthrauff and Jacob Medtart supplied his congregations, and it was doubtless under their administration that St. Paul's Church at Leitersburg was organized. The earliest list of members now extant, that of 1831, is as follows:

Daniel Beard,	Elizabeth Bell,
Mary Beckman,	Jacob E. Bell,
Andrew Bell,	John Bell, Jr.,

Mary Bell,
Catharine Bigham,
David Brant,
Caroline Burkhart,
Henrietta Burkhart,
Mary A. Burkhart,
Phoebe Burkhart,
Elizabeth Byer,
John Byer,
Susan Cole,
Barbara Cook,
Mary Cook,
Elizabeth Fletcher,
Louisa Frey,
Susanna Hartle,
Mary Hays,
Catharine Hoover,
John D. Kieffer,
Samuel Lahm,
Christian Lantz,
Elizabeth Lantz,
Samuel Lantz,
Ann Maria Leiter,
Barbara Leiter,
Barbara A. Leiter,
Catharine Leiter,
Elizabeth Leiter,
Isabella Leiter,
Samuel Leiter,
Susan Leiter,
Christian Lepley,
Catharine Lowman,
Mary A. Lowman,
Jacob Mangle,
Catharine Martin,
John Martin,
Catharine Metz,
James P. Mayhew,
Mary Mayhew,

Elizabeth Miller,
Elizabeth Mort,
John Nofford,
Joseph G. Protzman,
Sarah Protzman,
Catharine Repp,
John Repp,
Michael Repp,
Peter Repp,
Mary Ritter,
Jacob Ritter,
David Rook,
Joseph Ross,
Henry Ruthrauff,
Jacob Ruthrauff,
Susan Ruthrauff,
Mary A. Sheetz,
John Sheetz,
Frederick Schilling,
Julia A. Schilling,
John Shook,
Catharine Snider,
Henry Snider,
Elizabeth Spitzer,
Maria Stoff,
Catharine Tritle,
Lewis Tritle,
David Wolfinger,
Elizabeth Wolfinger,
Jacob Wolfinger,
Michael Wolfinger,
Sarah Wolfinger,
Henry Yesler,
Catharine Ziegler,
Frederick Ziegler,
George W. Ziegler,
Lewis Ziegler,
Magdalene Ziegler.

Among the members of the church council from 1835 to 1845 were Frederick Ziegler, Lewis Ziegler, John Byer, Jacob E. Bell, Samuel Lantz, Abner Hays, Henry H. Snider, Lewis Tritle, Samuel Creager, John Bowers, John Kissell, Jacob Wolfinger, Frederick Bell, George Bell, Jonas Bell, Samuel Etnyer, James P. Mayhugh, Jacob Kissell, and Thomas Atkinson.

The succession of pastors since the organization of the church has been as follows: Revs. John Ruthrauff, Jacob Medtart, and Benjamin Kurtz, D. D., 1825-28; Samuel K. Hoshour, 1828-30; John Reck, 1831-33; John P. Cline, 1833-46; John J. Riemensnyder, 1846-51; Daniel H. Bittle, D. D., 1851-52; J. F. Probst, 1853-56; John Heck, 1857-61; W. F. Eyster, D. D., 1861-65; M. C. Horine, D. D., 1865-69; Samuel McHenry, 1870-72; X. J. Richardson, 1872-81; Victor Miller, 1881—. Prior to 1828 the congregation was part of the Hagerstown charge, which embraced a wide extent of territory. From 1828 to 1880 it was part of the Smithsburg charge; the Leitersburg charge was formed in 1880 and embraces two congregations, Leitersburg and Beard's.

The site of the church and the burial ground adjacent, comprising lots Nos. 44 and 45 of the town plot of Leitersburg, were conveyed to Frederick Ziegler, John Byer, Jacob Bell, Lewis Tritle, John Bowers, and Henry H. Snider, who composed the church council, by John Lahm, February 28, 1835, at the consideration of $100.00.

A charter for the incorporation of the church was adopted on the 12th of April, 1864. The first trustees were Jacob E. Bell, Jonas Bell, John G. Garver, George Bell, Jacob Hoover, and James P. Mayhugh.

It has been stated that the corner-stone of the church was laid on the 6th of August, 1826; the kind of building it was proposed to erect was thus described in the following advertisement, which appeared in the Hagerstown *Torch-Light* some months before: "Proposals will be received until April 22d at the house of Christopher Burkhart in Leitersburg for building a church forty-five by sixty feet, two stories high, with gallery on three sides, to be built with brick or stone and rough-cast and finished in a plain, substantial manner." The building was evidently completed according to these specifications. It possessed no architectural pretensions, but was certainly one of the most substantial and commodious places of worship in Washington County. There was originally neither bell nor belfry, but about the year 1850 a bell was procured and mounted on a platform in the rear of the church; here it remained until 1853, when a belfry was built. In 1884-85 the building was completely remodeled at a cost of $4,100. A new front and tower were built, the side galleries were removed, the corresponding upper and lower windows were converted into one, the interior was refurnished, etc. The rededication occurred on the 1st of February, 1885, when an appropriate sermon was delivered by Rev. F. W. Conrad, D. D. The parsonage is a two-story brick structure, situated on the main street of the village. It was erected in 1881 at a cost of $3,100, and is jointly owned by the two congregations composing the charge. The site was presented by Rev. Victor Miller.

The Sunday school connected with this church was for many years a union school. It was organized soon after the erection of the church and has been continued without interruption to the present time.

The Woman's Home and Foreign Missionary Society was organized on the 15th of June, 1887, with ten constituent members and the following officers: President, Mrs. Josephine Miller; vice-president, Athalinda Bell; corresponding secretary, Mary E. Miller; recording secretary, Ida M. Bell; treasurer, Kate E. Martin.

The Young People's Society of Christian Endeavor was organized on the 22d of December, 1892, with the following officers: President, Mayberry G. Freed; vice-president, D. J. D. Hicks; corresponding secretary, Emma S. Newcomer; recording secretary, Mary E. Miller; treasurer, Frank D. Bell.

St. James' Reformed Church.

Among the early settlers of Leitersburg District there were several families that adhered to the Reformed faith, the most numerous and prominent of which were the Lamberts, Hartles, Schrivers, and Lecrons, all of whom, as evidenced by the records of Zion Reformed Church at Hagerstown, worshiped there and received the ministrations of its pastor in the ordinances of baptism, confirmation, etc. Other Reformed families located in the District at a later date, among which were those of Felix Beck, George Ziegler, Stephen Martin, Christian Russell, and John Harbaugh. After the erection of Beard's church at its present location this was the place of worship for adherents of the Reformed faith in Leitersburg District until 1826, when the first church at Leitersburg was built.

About the year 1826 two Reformed churches were organized

from the former constituency of Beard's, viz., Christ's at Cavetown and St. James' at Leitersburg. This was effected chiefly through the efforts of the Rev. Henry Kroh, who was the first pastor of both churches. Unfortunately, Mr. Kroh has left no local record of his work; but from the archives of the Maryland Classis it has been learned that he became pastor on the 15th of September, 1826; and on the 11th of June, 1827, the following action was taken by Classis:

Resolved, That the congregations of Cavetown and Leitersburg, Md., of which the Rev. Mr. Kroh is pastor, be received into connection with the Maryland Classis.

From September 15, 1826, to June 10, 1827, Mr. Kroh baptized 71, confirmed 55, buried 24; he reported 158 communicants and two schools. From June, 1827, to June, 1828, 132 were baptized, 65 confirmed, 44 buried; the number of communicants was 226. These statistics include both churches, and probably cover the period of Mr. Kroh's ministry.

In 1829 Rev. J. C. Bucher became pastor and Jacobs congregation in Harbaugh's valley was a third congregation in the charge. He resigned in 1830 and a vacancy followed, probably due to the inability of the charge to support a pastor. In 1831 Leitersburg and Cavetown were attached to the Waynesboro charge, then under the ministry of Rev. G. W. Glessner, D. D., who was succeeded in 1840 by Rev. J. H. A. Bomberger, D. D. Rev. Theodore Appel, D. D., became pastor in 1845. Two years later the extensive Waynesboro charge was divided and the Cavetown charge was established, its constituent congregations being those of Leitersburg, Cavetown, Harbaugh's in Franklin County, Pa., and Wolfsville in Frederick County, Md. Dr. Appel was the first pastor of the new charge, and continued in this relation until 1850. He was succeeded by Rev. J. W. Santee, D. D., who preached his first sermon at Leitersburg on the 4th of May, 1851, and continued as pastor forty-one years and six months. His son and successor, Rev. Charles A. Santee, was pastor from 1892 until May, 1896, when the present incumbent, Rev. S. H. Dietzel, was called. His pastorate began on the 1st of January, 1897. The congregations at Cavetown, Leitersburg, and Wolfsville constitute the charge, Harbaugh's Church having been detached some years ago. The pastoral residence is at Cavetown.

In the summer of 1826 the Rev. Henry Kroh preached to his congregation in a grove near the village school house where the buildings are now located on the farm of George H. Wolfinger, formerly owned by Solomon Hartle.

For a period of nearly forty years, closing with 1866, the Reformed congregation worshiped in the Lutheran church, to the original erection of which its membership had made substantial contributions. From the 1st of January to the 18th of August, 1867, there was no Reformed service in Leitersburg. The use of the United Brethren church was then secured, and here services were regularly held until 1879. The erection of a church edifice was agitated in 1868, but the project never passed the initial stage. In the spring of 1878 another effort was made, resulting in the present edifice. Formal action in this direction was first taken at a congregational meeting on the 5th of August, when articles of incorporation and a constitution for the government of the congregation were adopted, and a building committee was selected composed of Peter Middlekauff, Jacob Hartle, Solomon Hartle, John H. Miller, J. Freeland Leiter, John Middlekauff, and Rev. J. W. Santee, D. D. An acre of ground for church site and burial purposes was purchased from Joseph Barkdoll. On the 20th of August the committee decided to erect a brick building sixty feet long and thirty-five feet wide, with tower ten feet square; the general supervision of the work was entrusted to J. Freeland Leiter and Peter Middlekauff. The corner-stone was laid on the 19th of September, 1878, and the consecration occurred on the 16th of March, 1879. On the latter occasion the sermon was delivered by Rev. J. O. Miller, D. D., of York, Pa.; Dr. Santee and Rev. S. S. Miller were also present. Services were also held on three successive evenings of the following week, when the officiating clergymen were Revs. J. Spangler Kieffer, D. D., I. N. Motter, and F. F. Bahner. On the 30th of March, 1879, the churchyard was consecrated to the purposes of Christian burial. At that time the consistory was composed of Peter Middlekauff and Jacob Hartle, elders; John H. Miller and Jacob A. Ziegler, deacons.

The Sunday school was organized on the 20th of April, 1884, with the following officers: Superintendent, J. D. Lambert; assistant superintendent, B. F. Spessard; secretary, Emma Barnhart; treasurer, J. P. Middlekauff. The first teachers were Emma Barnhart, J. A. Strite, J. D. Lambert, Alice Ziegler, Abigail Ziegler, Mrs. Catharine Miller, and Mrs. Rebecca Bowers. The number of scholars at the organization was thirty-five. The succession of superintendents has been as follows: J. D. Lambert, Clinton Hartle, John Summer, Iva Spessard, Harry Wolfinger, and Thomas Summer.

MILLER'S MENNONITE CHURCH.

There was a considerable number of Mennonites among the early settlers of Washington County. In 1776-77 they were a subject of consideration by the County Committee of Observation, as they declined to take up arms or participate in military exercises. Although excused from actual service they were required to furnish transportation and supplies for the county troops, to make contributions in money, and to assist the families of those who were in the army.

Among the early settlers of Leitersburg District who adhered to the Mennonite faith was Jacob Good, a resident near the Little Antietam as early as 1765. It is supposed that his immediate neighbors, Michael Miller and Andrew Reiff, were also Mennonites, but this can not be positively stated. John Barr, Jacob Miller, and John Strite, all of whom were Mennonites, located in the District prior to 1800, and Christian Shank in 1812. Among the most prominent and numerous Mennonite families in the adjacent Districts were the Shanks, Newcomers, Hoovers, Bachtels, Hoffmans, Weltys, and Eshlemans.

For many years the Mennonites in this part of Washington County met for public worship at private houses. It is an established fact that the stone house on the farm of Abraham H. Martin in Cavetown District, built in 1820 by Henry Shank, was a regular place of meeting for some years. On the Loose farm near Fiddlersburg stands a building erected many years ago by Martin Bachtel, who owned the farm at that time and was an influential member of the Mennonite connection, in which he held the office of minister. This building was used as a place of worship until the year 1835, when Miller's church in Leitersburg District was built. The original list of subscriptions for this purpose is still preserved and reads as follows:

December den 25ten, 1834.

Wir, die unterschriebenen zu dieser subscription, versprechen zu bezahlen an Christian Shank, Jacob Miller, und Johannes Strite oder an einer von den oben benahmten oder au ihre Verordnete die Sum oder Sumen zu unsere Namen gezeiget wie unden folget, zur Abstattung der unkosten vom Bau einem Mennonischen Gemeinhaus welches gebaut werden soll in Washington County nahe bei Leitersburg auf ein Stuck Land vorhin zu Jacob Miller und hetz dass Eigenthum von der oben gemeldete Gemeinde.

Martin Bachtel,
John Strite,
Christian Shank,
Jacob Miller,
John Eshleman,
Abraham Stouffer,
Peter Newcomer,
Andrew Shank,
Jacob Shank,
Andrew and Jacob Newcomer,
Daniel Shank,
Christian Stouffer,
Abraham Stouffer, Jr.,
John Newcomer.
Christian Newcomer,
Benjamin Garver.
Lewis Ziegler,
Jonas Shank,
Samuel Strite,
Henry Snively,
Andrew Snively,
John Welty,
George H. Lambert,
John Lesher,
John Horst,
Joseph Reiff, Sr.,
Christian Barr,

Jacob Barr,
Henry Funk,
Abraham Strite,
John Byer,
John Snively,
George Poe,
Jacob Funk,
Samuel Bachtel,
Joseph Strite,
Christian Strite,
Daniel Scheetz,
Joseph Gabby,
William Gabby,
John Hoover,
Andrew Shank,
Christopher Burkhart,
Samuel Lantz,
Jacob Bell,
Garrett Wolff,
Frederick Bell,
Frederick Byer,
Henry Schriver,
Peter Hoover,
Jacob Hoffman,
David Hoover,
Jacob Lesher,
George Shiess.

The German may be translated as follows:

We, the undersigned to this subscription, promise to pay to Christian Shank, Jacob Miller, and John Strite or any one of them or to their order the sum or sums marked opposite our names as follows below, to pay the cost of building a Mennonite meeting house which shall be built in Washington County near to Leitersburg upon a piece of ground at Jacob Miller's and to be the exclusive property of the above mentioned congregation.

On the 25th of March, 1835, Christian Shank, Jacob Miller, and John Strite entered into a contract with Joseph Cookston for the erection of "a stone meeting house on Jacob Miller's farm." It was specified that the building should be forty feet long and thirty feet wide, "laid off in three different apartments," with two chimneys, "a sufficient number of doors, windows, tables, benches," etc.; that Cookston should "procure at his own proper expense all the necessary materials and of a good quality" and finish the building by the 1st of July; and that he should receive the sum of $510. The contract was duly executed and the building thus erected constitutes the main part of the present place of worship. In 1888 an addition of twenty feet was built under the supervision of a committee composed of John Strite, Joseph Eshleman, and David Strite. The present building is therefore sixty feet in length.

The church grounds originally comprised half an acre, the deed for which was executed on the 4th of April, 1835. An additional purchase of 125 perches was made in 1869 and one of seventeen perches in 1889.

The first trustees were Christian Shank, John Strite, and Jacob Miller. The following is a list of their successors: Christian Strite, elected August 9, 1845, *vice* John Strite, deceased; Christian Horst, elected May 1, 1856, *vice* Christian Shank, deceased; Joseph Eshleman and Frederick Shank, elected December 6, 1862, *vice* Christian Strite, deceased, and Christian Horst, who had removed out of the bounds of the congregation; Joseph Strite, elected January 30, 1864, *vice* Frederick Shank, deceased; John Miller, elected December 26, 1868, *vice* John Miller, deceased; John S. Strite, elected November 27, 1890, *vice* Joseph Eshleman, deceased; Jacob Eshleman, elected October 25, 1891, *vice* Joseph Strite, deceased; Christian Eshleman, elected June 9, 1893, *vice* John Miller, deceased. The present trustees are Jacob Eshleman, John S. Strite, and Christian Eshleman.

Among the first ministers who preached at this church were Peter Eshleman, Christian Newcomer, John Welty, Christian Strite, John Martin, and Jacob Oberholtzer. The present ministers are Adam Baer, Henry Baer, and John C. Miller.

The first bishop who officiated at Miller's church was Abraham Roth, of Mummasburg, Adams County, Pa., whose successors have been Peter Eshleman and Michael Horst. Bishop Horst's jurisdiction embraces all the Mennonite Churches in Washington County.

The Sunday-school was organized in 1893 with Adam Baer as the first superintendent. John C. Miller held this office in 1894-96, and Adam Baer in 1897.

LONGMEADOWS GERMAN BAPTIST CHURCH.

The Longmeadows or Rowland's German Baptist Church is not an individual organization, but an integral part of the Beaver Creek congregation. The membership of this communion residing north of Hagerstown, having a long distance to travel to attend the services of their church at Beaver Creek, met occasionally for worship at Paradise school house and also at private houses. Jonas Rowland was among those who realized the importance of having a permanent place of worship, and in 1853 he erected at his own expense a brick church building. He burned the brick on his own farm, from which the church site was also donated. After the completion of the building he was partially reimbursed by his fellow-members. This building was forty feet long and thirty-five feet wide, and occupied the site of the present structure. In 1881 it was removed, when the present place of worship was erected. This also is a brick building, of which the respective dimensions are forty and seventy feet. It was erected under the supervision of a building committee composed of George W. Petre, Andrew J. Boward, and Daniel N. Scheller. In 1896 a frame dwelling house was built adjacent to the church for the occupancy of the sexton.

The membership of the German Baptist Church in this locality in 1853 included George Petre, Jonas Rowland and wife, David Rowland, Daniel Rowland, George W. Petre, Amy Petre, Margaret Petre, Henry Shank and wife, Mrs. Crumb, Joseph Wolf and wife, Mrs. Philip Warfield, David Anthony and wife, George Poe, Samuel Trovinger, Andrew Boward, Sr., and wife, and others. The first ministers were Joseph Wolf, Henry Koons, Jacob Hilbarger, and Joseph Emmert, who were succeeded by Leonard Emmert, Andrew Cost, Daniel F. Stouffer, Barton Shoup, Frederick D. Anthony, Abram Rowland, and John Rowland, of whom Elders Shoup, Abram Rowland, and

John Rowland are the present ministers. The bishop in 1853 was Henry Koons, who was succeeded by Andrew Cost and Daniel F. Stouffer. In the board of trustees for the Beaver Creek congregation Longmeadows is represented by Daniel N. Scheller and George W. Petre.

By the will of Henry Shank of Antrim Township, who died in 1875, the sum of $500 was bequeathed to this congregation.

The Sunday school at Rowland's was organized in 1893. A union Sunday school had previously been conducted at Paradise school house, of which the school at Rowland's may be regarded as a continuation, as it is also a union school. Elder John Rowland was superintendent in 1893 and 1894. In 1895 the school was not organized. The superintendent in 1896 and 1897 was John Rowe.

Reformed Mennonite.

For more than half a century Reformed Mennonite services have been regularly held at intervals of two months at Paradise school house. The ministers of the Waynesboro congregation usually preach here, with others from Chambersburg and elsewhere.

River Brethren.

Daniel Jacobs, who located near the terminus of the Marsh turnpike, was a member of the River Brethren Church, and public worship was regularly held for many years at his house and that of his son-in-law, Jacob Hykes. Among the ministers who conducted these services were Henry Myers, Martin Stoner, John Hawbecker, Christopher Hoover, John Hoover, and Christopher Breckbill.

United Brethren Church, Leitersburg.

This organization had its origin in religious services at the house of Peter Stotler, on the Little Antietam near Leitersburg and now the property of Joseph and John B. Barkdoll. Here prayer and class meetings were regularly held, with preaching at intervals by the itinerant ministers of the denomination. Among the first members were Peter Stotler, Henry Yesler, John Miller, Jacob Dayhoff, Adam Bovey, and their families, who were succeeded at a later date by Henry Boertner, John D. Eakle, John and Peter Yesler, and John Dayhoff. About the year 1835 a church edifice was built at Leitersburg; a parsonage was also secured and for some years the church prospered. Its membership was gradually reduced by death and removal, however, and finally the church building was sold and the congregation disbanded.

METHODIST EPISCOPAL CHURCH, LEITERSBURG.

Among the leading members of this church were Edward Smith, who afterwards entered the ministry, John Johnson, the local class-leader, Jonathan Humphreys, and John Brown. The village school house was their first place of worship, and about the year 1841 a brick church was built by Alexander Hamilton and Henry Smith of Waynesboro, Pa. It is now the residence of Mrs. Ida Leather. The pastors of the Waynesboro circuit preached here until 1857, after which services were occasionally conducted by Rev. Henry Stonehouse of that place until the society disbanded.

CEMETERIES.

One of the earliest places of interment in Washington County was the burial ground adjacent to Antietam church. Interments were made here as early as 1763.

There are a number of private burial grounds in Leitersburg District, and here many of the pioneers sleep their last sleep. The earliest mortuary inscription that the writer has discovered appears on a stone in a private burial ground on the farm of Joseph Martin. It reads as follows: "1781. Hier liegt Eva Lambert und ihre Tochter. War alt 59 Jahr." A short distance from the Greencastle road on a slope toward the Antietam there is a burial ground inclosed by a substantial brick wall erected by J. F. Leiter and L. Z. Leiter in 1896. Andrew Leiter, the founder of Leitersburg, Jacob Leiter, his father, who died in 1814, and other early members of the Leiter family are interred here. It is not improbable that this is also the burial place of the first Jacob Leiter, who died in 1764. Southwest of Leitersburg on the farm of George F. Ziegler is the Ziegler burial ground, where some of the early representatives of the Lantz, Ziegler, and other families are interred. This was a place of burial as early as 1783. It is surrounded by a brick wall, erected in 1889 by George W., David, and Sophia Ziegler. The Hartle burial ground, on the farm of Alveh L. Stockslager, is inclosed by a substantial stone wall. The burial ground of the Lecron family is situated on the farm of John D. Spessard; that of the Good and Barr families, on the farm of C. L. G. Anderson; of the Gilberts and Rowlands, on that of Daniel N. Scheller; of the Garvers, on that of William H. Hoffman; of the Dayhoffs, on that of William H. Stevenson. There are also private burial grounds on the farms of Upton Clopper, Samuel Cook, etc.

A burial ground is connected with each of the five churches of the District. That at Jacobs is the oldest, and here there are many graves marked by rough headstones bearing no inscriptions whatever. It may be positively stated, however, that interments were made here as early as 1790.

CHAPTER V.

SCHOOLS.

"THE HOLLOW HOUSE" — MARTIN'S SCHOOL — LEITERSBURG SCHOOLS—THE JACOBS CHURCH SCHOOL—"JACOB MILLER'S SCHOOL HOUSE"—PARADISE—ROCK HILL—PLEASANT HILL— NEW HARMONY—MT. UNION—GENERAL STATISTICS.

IT is difficult to trace the history of early educational effort in Leitersburg District. It may be positively stated that George Adam Mueller was a teacher in the Jacobs church neighborhood in 1774 and Michael Boor in 1786, but where they taught is a matter of conjecture. The population of the District was certainly ample to sustain one or more schools as early as the Revolution, but while it is highly probable that the more enterprising and intelligent among the pioneers secured for their children some local educational advantages, no record of such efforts has been preserved.

"THE HOLLOW HOUSE."

One of the earliest school houses of the District stood on the north side of the Greencastle road about a mile from Leitersburg and a short distance from the residence of Andrew Strite. From its location in a deep depression between two hills this was long known and is still remembered as "the hollow house." The building has been removed, and but little now remains to mark its location except a well of water. It was a long, low structure, built of logs, and served both as school room and as residence for the teacher. Here Thomas Hauks taught in 1804. The following correspondence, the original of which is preserved by Mark Z. Poe of Leitersburg, is probably the earliest document extant relating to the educational history of the District:

SIR: As the first quarter was to have been in advance there could be no doubt of its being due now, but as I did not stand in any great need of the money till now I did not think it material to write you for any; but my family as well as myself being at this time in a bad state of health make it indispensably necessary that I should write you this note, the purport of which is for the sum of $4.00, which you will please to send by one of your sons in the morning when they come to school, for which I will send you a receipt in the evening of the same day.

July 24, 1804. THOMAS HAUKS.
Mr. George Ziegler.

Charles Cavender taught here in 1813 and a Mr. Crawford about 1820. The latter appears to have been one of the last teachers. There can be little doubt that this school was established prior to 1800, and that a large part of the District was embraced in its territory.

MARTIN'S SCHOOL.

One mile east of Leitersburg on the main road to Smithsburg is the school house locally known as Longmeadows or Martin's. On the opposite side of the road from the present modern building stands a long, one-story, wooden structure, weather-beaten and dilapidated though still comparatively substantial. This building may well be regarded as a landmark in the educational history of the District. From the original subscription paper for its erection it is learned that "a number of the inhabitants of Upper Antietam Hundred in Washington County, Md., met according to notice given for that purpose at the dwelling house of Christian Good on the 2d of March last [1811] in order to choose suitable persons and a proper place for building a school house and the persons then and there met did unanimously elect Christian Good, John Moyer, and Jacob Lambert trustees for carrying into effect the said purpose," who accordingly selected "a lot of ground on a corner of Christian Good's plantation, on which they provided material and commenced the building." This they agreed to finish "with good and sufficient materials and in a neat and workmanlike manner, the whole to be made with two good floors and well illuminated with glass windows, the room for a school to be furnished with a desk, two writing tables, with proper seats and a good stove. The part intended for the accommodation of a teacher and family is also to be well furnished with a good stone chimney, door, windows," etc. It was further specified "that the said house shall be and remain for the sole use of a school and accommodation of a teacher and for no other purpose, except that it be open on Sundays and other convenient

MILLER'S CHURCH.

days, and it is agreed that is shall be freely open to any society of Christians who meet for public worship."

The cost of the building was $322.96, and a second subscription was necessary before the entire amount was provided for. The lease for the ground was executed by Good to Lambert and Moyer on the 4th of January, 1817. In this instrument the site is described as located "on the main road leading from Greencastle to Harman's Gap." The dimensions of the plat were seventy and forty-four feet, respectively, from which it is evident that very meager provision was made for a play-ground. The lease was to terminate April 1, 1896—eighty years "from the first day of April now last past." The annual rental was twenty-five cents, which was paid for some years—probably until the death of Stephen Martin, who purchased the Good farm in 1817. The lease describes the school house as "substantial and well furnished." It was to be used "for the exclusive purpose of education, and occasionally on Sabbath or holidays or other suitable days for divine worship." The sale of "beer, ale, or other liquors" and the holding of "any offensive entertainment" were forbidden.

Thomas Smith was teacher in 1819, and probably for some years prior to that date. He resided in the school building. The last teacher who did so was probably Francis Shiess. Among the successors of the original trustees were George M. Boyer, Jacob Garver, and John Oswald, who held office in 1828; Jacob Shank, who succeeded Oswald in 1828, and Peter Newcomer, who succeeded Shank in 1830; Andrew Shank, Jr., Jacob E. Bell, and David Bell, 1840.

The Jacobs Church School.

The school house at Jacobs church was situated about the center of the graveyard, where a ledge of rocks rendered the ground unsuitable for burial purposes. It was a one-story log building, nearly square, and was divided into two apartments by a wooden partition. The apartment on the south side constituted the residence of the teacher, while the other was used for school purposes. The latter was entered from the east side; there was a window opposite the door and two on the north side. The walls were neither plastered nor wainscoted. The furniture consisted of a ten-plate stove in the center of the room; the teacher's desk, which occupied one corner by the door; a writing desk for girls, opposite the entrance, and one for boys, along the north side; and several long slab benches without backs. The benches for the girls were placed close to the partition and parallel with it, so that they could sit with some degree of comfort, but no provision of this kind was enjoyed by the boys.

It is possible that this school was established about the time the church was organized (1791), but this is improbable. John Elliot taught in the Jacobs church neighborhood in 1810 and in 1817 (January 6th) Charles Cavender gave to Henry Jacobs a receipt for $2.00 "in full of subscription to school house." It is probable that this school house was at Jacobs church, and that it was erected in 1816 or 1817. It is believed that German teachers were at first employed, among the last of whom was a Mr. Beaver, who subsequently removed to Ohio. John McKee was the teacher for some years and occupied the teacher's quarters in the school building; unlike many of his pedagogical associates, who itinerated from one community to another, he became a permanent resident of this locality, acquired a modest home near Antietam Junction, and lived there until his death. He was a native Scotchman and a man of fine education, but while his ability was recognized he never became popular with the German constituency at Jacobs church. Although the adoption of the public school system in Pennsylvania deprived this school of a large share of its former patronage it was sustained with varying success until about the year 1854. The building was then converted into a dwelling for the sexton of the church and served this purpose until finally demolished.

Leitersburg Schools.

Joseph Gabby, who was born near Leitersburg in 1779, used to relate that in his boyhood he attended a school near his home, at which nearly all his fellow pupils were from German families. It would be interesting to know more about this school, but further information seems unattainable, unless it may be identified with "the hollow house."

After the founding of the village a local school became a public necessity, and a log building was accordingly erected for this purpose on the north side of the turnpike a short distance west of the village. The site was then owned by John Barr and is now embraced in the Wolfinger farm. About the year 1840 it was destroyed by fire and replaced by a brick building, which was used for school purposes until the erection of the present building. It was then demolished, but the materials still serve an educational function, having been utilized in the erection of the Spessard school house on the Chewsville road. Neither of these buildings possessed much architectural merit. In the first the logs were untrimmed at the corners, which gave it a ragged, backwoods appearance.

In 1825 the local school authorities published the following advertisement in a Hagerstown newspaper:

A Teacher Wanted.

A man of steady habits, who is well qualified to teach the various branches of a good English education, will meet with an agreeable situation at Leitersburg. None need apply but such as can furnish testimonials of character, etc.

William Gabby,
Frederick Ziegler,
John Barr,
Lewis Ziegler.

August 10, 1825. *Trustees.*

Among the early teachers at Leitersburg were Messrs. Winrode, Chancellor, and McGeechan; Samuel Brown, subsequently a successful physician at Philadelphia; and J. Allen Brown, who afterward became an eminent divine and was for many years a member of the faculty of the Lutheran Theological Seminary at Gettysburg.

Three teachers are employed in the Leitersburg schools, in which the respective departments are designated as grammar, intermediate, and primary. The school building is a substantial brick structure and occupies an elevated location with ample grounds. It comprises three rooms, two of which constitute the main building, erected in 1868-69, and here the grammar and intermediate departments are conducted; an extension in the rear was subsequently built for the primary department.

"Jacob Miller's School House."

This school house was situated in the immediate vicinity of Miller's church, directly in the rear of the dwelling house on the farm of Noah E. Shank, and was probably built or used for school purposes after the school at "the hollow house" had been discontinued. John Davis taught here in 1823 and Joseph Miller in 1827. Thomas Banks was the teacher in the spring of 1829 and Hilary Herbert in the winter of 1829-30. Banks's contract with his patrons specified that they should provide for him "a good and sufficient school house furnished with a good and suitable stove and a number of benches; also a supply of fuel delivered at the school house door." For every child put under his care "to teach them reading, writing, and arithmetic" he was to receive $8.00 per year. He agreed "to attend his school at regular hours and to progress his pupils in their respective studies as fast as possible." The agreement is dated March 5, 1829; "School to commence on the 1st day of April next in Jacob Miller's school house."

Paradise.

Formal action for the erection of a school house in the Paradise district was taken at a public meeting on the 15th of October, 1829, at which Jacob Schmutz presided and Thomas H. Rench was secretary. George Arendt, Joseph Trovinger, and Daniel Schlencker were elected trustees for the prospective District; Jacob Schmutz and Elisha Harne were appointed to solicit subscriptions; and it was decided "to build a school house on the cross-roads of stone twenty-five feet square by the subscribers for the benefit of the neighborhood." Four days later (October 19th) Daniel Schlencker, one of the trustees, entered into a contract with John Newman by which the latter obligated himself "to build a school house of stone, twenty-five feet square, eight feet high, and the walls twenty inches" at the rate of eighty-five and one-half cents per perch. It was further specified that the building should have a chimney and "one rough coat" of plaster. The contractor also agreed to quarry the stone. In 1832 Henry Schlencker executed a deed to the trustees conveying a plot of ground "at the intersection of the roads leading from Hagerstown and Waynesboro and Schmutz's mill and the Greencastle road"— "East with the Greencastle road, one hundred feet; north with the Hagerstown and Waynesboro road, sixty-five feet"—"for the purpose of building a church or school house" and at the consideration of $5.00.

SCHOOLS.

The building was probably erected in the spring of 1830. In the course of his professional rounds Dr. Frederick Dorsey passed one day while building operations were in progress and made some inquiries of the workmen regarding the purpose of the structure upon which they were engaged. He was told that it was to be a school house, and asked whether any name had yet been selected. This was answered in the negative. "Call it Paradise," said the Doctor, as he drove away. The name at once received popular approval and has since enjoyed undisputed currency.

The first subscription having proven inadequate a second paper was circulated, in which it was stated that the trustees "have succeeded in erecting a large and comfortable house (being situated where the road from Hagerstown to Waynesboro crosses a road generally known by the name of the Schmutz mill road) and bearing the title of the 'Paradise school and meeting house;' that they have furnished a sufficient number of desks and benches, also a large ten-plate stove; that it is public for religious sects of all denominations."

Notwithstanding the importunities of the solicitors, there was still a considerable balance unpaid on the 31st of January, 1835.

Some years after the completion of this building the gable wall showed a disposition to part company with the remainder of the structure, and in order to avert such a catastrophe several heavy timbers were propped against it. In course of time the timbers rotted away, but the wall, contrary to all expectations, obstinately refused to fall. The general condition of the building, however, eventually became so dilapidated that an effort was made to replace it with a new one and subscriptions were solicited for this purpose by Captain Henry Clopper and George Petre. On a Saturday evening in the autumn of 1853 a meeting of citizens was held at the school house to consider the project. It was found that the amount subscribed was only about half the cost of the contemplated new building. in consequence of which the project was practically abandoned, when George Petre arose and said it was a shame the community could not afford a better school house for its children; he offered to double his subscription, others agreed to do the same, and it was at once decided to rebuild. On the following Monday and Tuesday the old stone house was demolished; on Wednesday the bricks were hauled, and on Thursday the erection of the present building was begun. It was completed in time for occupancy the ensuing winter and has since been used for school purposes.

Among the first teachers at Paradise were James Gallion, Jacob Lightcap, Henry Leiter, Michael Feierstein, George Carson, Samuel Phillips, and Gearhart Brenner.

ROCK HILL.

The first school house at Rock Hill was built in 1831. George I. Harry, the owner of Colebrook farm at that time, donated a log house that stood on his estate; it was demolished and rebuilt by the united exertions of the community and constituted the first school house at Rock Hill. The first teacher was James Gelwix, whose services were secured by Mr. Harry, and who is said to have possessed qualifications superior to those of the average country pedagogue at that day. The first trustees were Jacob Miller, George I. Harry, Abraham Strite, Peter Eshleman, Christian Strite, and Samuel Strite, to whom the school grounds were leased by John Strite for the term of forty years from the 1st of April, 1831. In 1858 this lease was superseded by a deed, executed by Jacob Miller in favor of Abraham Strite, John Miller, and Joseph Eshleman, trustees, under whose supervision the present school house was erected in the same year. It is a substantial brick building and has been continuously used for school purposes.

PLEASANT HILL.

The first school within the present limits of Pleasant Hill district was taught in 1806-07 by the Rev. Jacob Dayhoff at his residence on the farm of William H. Stevenson. A German school was subsequently taught at a log house near the farm buildings of William H. Hoffman.

About the year 1830 the community united in the erection of a log school building on the land of John Mentzer. It stood on the Ringgold road on the hill above the present residence of Mrs. Mary M. Newcomer. Among those who taught here were Mrs. Anna (Snively) Garver, Rev. Christian Lepley of the Lutheran Church, and several members of the Mentzer family. In 1852 or '53 this building was removed and rebuilt at the location of

SCHOOLS.

the present school house, the site of which was leased by John D. Eakle to Benjamin Garver, Daniel Winter, and Samuel Nigh on the 8th of February, 1853. This instrument contained a reversionary clause in favor of the grantor and his heirs in case the ground should cease to be used for school purposes, and in 1877, when the present brick school building was erected, it was superseded by a deed vesting the title in the county school board.

NEW HARMONY.

The New Harmony school house is a substantial brick building and was erected by public subscription. The first trustees were Henry Schriver, David Gilbert, and Daniel Mentzer, to whom Joseph Strite executed a deed for sixty-four perches of land, December 17, 1855. An additional purchase of sixty perches was made in 1885, when the course of the public road was changed to permit the enlargement of the school grounds. The title to the property is still vested in a local board of trustees. The county school board pays an annual rental, which is expended upon repairs and improvements.

MT. UNION.

This district was created by the county school board in 1868, when a brick school house was erected. The first teacher was John O. Wolfinger, by whom the school was opened in January, 1869. The present school house was built in 1890.

GENERAL STATISTICS.

In 1824 the managers of the school fund in District No. 7 (Cavetown), which embraced the village of Leitersburg and a large part of the District, were William H. Fitzhugh, Peter Seibert, William Gabby, John Welty, and Marmaduke W. Boyd. District No. 7 received $44.00 from the county school fund, from which it is evident that the duties of the commissioners were not onerous. The county school fund in 1825 was $450, of which District No. 7 received $65.00.

In 1845 the trustees of the school fund in District No. 9 were Lewis Ziegler, John Mentzer, George I. Harry, George Kessinger, Jr., and Abraham Stouffer. Abraham Strite served as school commissioner from 1849 to 1851 and Samuel Etnyer in 1852-53.

In 1853 there were eight schools in the District, with 276 paying scholars and 16 free scholars; the amount received from the county school fund was $509.32 and from tuition fees $520.26. In 1849, according to the official report of Abraham Strite, the books and supplies at each school within the present limits of the District (Martin's excepted) were as follows:

Leitersburg.—Thirty-four spellers, 18 American Manuals, 15 grammars, 400 quills, 100 slate pencils, 1 register, 21 arithmetics, 22 dictionaries, 34 McGuffey's readers, 8 Elements of Agriculture.

Pleasant Hill.—Thirty spelling books, 8 grammars, 11 geographies, 6 inkstands, 100 slate pencils, 200 quills, 1 register, 15 arithmetics, 18 dictionaries, 18 copy-books, 100 quills, 9 copy-books, 4 Elements of Agriculture, 18 McGuffey's readers.

Jacobs Church.—Twelve dictionaries, 36 Comly Spelling Books, 16 arithmetics, 4 grammars, 6 geographies, 6 large slates, 100 quills, 4 Elements of Agriculture, 30 McGuffey's readers.

Paradise.—Twelve copy-books, 5 quires of paper, 12 American Manuals, 6 Chandler's Grammars, 38 Comly Spelling Books, 100 slate pencils, 2 quarts of ink, 14 arithmetics, 6 dictionaries, 12 slates, 8 geographies, 1 register, 18 McGuffey's readers.

Rock Hill.—Fifteen Comly Spelling Books, 13 arithmetics, 6 American Manuals, 3 grammars, 3 geographies, 12 copy-books, 100 quills, 2 dictionaries, 6 elements of Agriculture, 18 McGuffey's readers, 2 slates, 1 register.

INDEX

___, Elizabeth, 121
Gabby, ___, 51
Adams, Jacob, 83
Adams, John Quincy, 129
Allen, Capt., 65
Allison, Patrick, 78
Altig, Michael, 119
Anderson, C. L. G., 27, 35, 142
Anderson, Freeland W., 86, 99, 101, 105
Anderson, William, 66, 107
Anthony, David, 139
Anthony, Frederick D, 139
Appel, Theodore, 134
Arendt, George, 150
Armour, Charkes A. (Mrs), 104, 106
Atkinson, Thomas, 106, 131
Augenstein, George, 119
Avet, Abram, 66
Avey, Samuel 67
Avey, Abram, 66
Bachman, Andrew, 81, 103, 106
Bachtel, Martin, 58, 136, 137
Bachtel, Samuel, 65, 137
Baer, Adam, 138, 139
Baer, Henry, 138
Bahner, F. F., 135
Baker, ___, 15
Baker, B. F., 111
Baker, Benjamin, 83
Baker, Benjamin F., 36, 37
Baker, George, 119
Baker, George, Jr., 119
Baker, Peter, 81, 85
Baker's mill, 73
Ball, Anthony, 119
Baltimore, Lord, 45
Banks, Thomas, 150
Barkdoll, ___, 40, 96
Barkdoll, John B., 37, 140
Barkdoll, Joseph, 31

Barkdoll, Joseph S.,
Barkdoll, Henry, 33, 50
Barkdoll, John B., 101, 140
Barkdoll, Joseph, 101, 102, 104, 135, 140
Barkdoll, Joseph S., 111
Barkdoll, William, 40
Barkdoll, John B., 140
Barnhart, David, 68, 104, 106, 107, 111,
Barnhart, Henry, 104
Barnhart, Emma, 135, 136
Barr, Christian, 137
Barr family, 95
Barr, John, 26, 27, 53, 72, 136, 149
Barr, Jacob, 38, 137
Barr, Jacob H., 84
Barr, Martin, 27
Barrs, ___, 35
Beard, ___, 115
Beard, Daniel, 130
Beard, Dr., 115
Beard, George, 84
Beard, Isaac G., 85
Beard, John, 114
Beard, William, 43, 44
Beaver, John, 105, 125
Beaver, Mr., 148
Beck, Felix, 94, 133
Beckman, John, 105, 107
Beckman, Mary, 130
Bell, Andrew, 37, 53, 106, 119, 139
Bell, Anthony, 33, 39, 43, 118, 119, 120
Bell, Athalinda, 133
Bell, Daniel, 70, 126
Bell, David, 60, 147
Bell, Elizabeth, 130
Bell, Ernest E., 126
Bell, Frank D., 62, 107, 133
Bell, Frederick, 34, 53, 62, 84, 88, 89, 94, 121, 125, 130, 137

Bell, Frederick, Jr., 101
Bell, George, 70, 91, 132
Bell, Henry F., 71
Bell, Ida M., 121, 124
Bell, Jacob, 57, 132, 137
Bell, Jacob E., 28, 60, 83, 84, 88, 89, 108, 130, 131, 132, 147
Bell, Johannes, 121
Bell, John, 119, 129
Bell, John, Jr., 130
Bell, John A., 35
Bell, Jones, 132
Bell, Joseph M., 33, 46, 126
Bell, L. J., 124
Bell, Margaret, 37, 101
Bell, Margaretha, 121
Bell, Mary, 131
Bell, Peter, 33, 43, 60, 72, 84, 118
Bell, Philip M., 67
Bell, Rosina, 121
Bell, Joseph M. (Mrs), 126
Bell, Upton, 105, 107
Bell, Johannes, 121
Belt, Thomas, 39, 55, 54, 56, 62, 99
Beltzhoover, Melchoir, 34
Bergstresser, P., 124, 125
Besore, Jeremiah S., 84
Besore, Charles H., 68, 106
Besore, David, 119
Besore, Joseph, 106
Bidwell, John, 61
Bigham, Catharine, 131
Bigham, Robert, 88
Bishop, Elijah, 84
Bittle, Daniel H., 132
Blackburn, Elizabeth, 114
Blackburn, Robert, 114
Blaine, James G., 61
Boertner, Henry, 141
Bomberger, J. H. A.,
Bomberger, Rev, 124, 126
Bonebrake, John, 49
Boner, John, 67
Boone, George, 17
Boone, William, 17
Boor, Michael, 143

Bouquet, Col., 90, 100
Bouquet, Henry, 22, 23, 63, 90, 100
Bovey, Adam, 140
Boward, Andrew J., 139
Boward, Andrew, Sr., 139
Bowers, A. H.
Bowers, John, 131, 132
Bowers, Rebecca, 135
Bowers, A. H., 107
Bowman, George H., 68. 81, 94
Bowman's mill, 84, 87, 99
Boyd, Mr., 83
Boyd, Marmaduke W., 83, 153
Boyer, George M, 147
Boyer, Philip, 33, 34
Brant, David, 131
Breckbill, Christopher, 140
Brenner, Gearhart, 152
Brown, I. G., 84
Brown, Ignatius, 60
Brown, J. Allen, 149
Brown, John, 12, 141
Brown, Samuel, 149
Brumbaugh, David, 60, 84, 93
Brumbaugh, Henry, 60
Brumbaugh, Jacob, 73
Brumbaugh's mill, 89
Brunett, Michael, 106
Bryan, Alexander, 47
Bryan, Mr., 47
Bryan, William J., 61
Bryson, Charles, 55
Buchanan, Benjamin, 55
Bucher, J. C., 134
Buhrman, Alfred, 125
Burger, Emanuel, 90
Burkhart, Caroline, 131
Burkart, Christopher, 30, 36, 37, 44, 62, 63, 72, 74, 87, 91, 104, 106, 119, 130, 137
Burkhart, Christopher, Jr., 119
Burkhart, George, 74, 119
Burkhart, Henrietta, 131
Burkhart, Mary A, 131
Burkhart, Phoebe, 131
Burkart's mill, 79, 91

Burkhart's hotel, 106
Burkhart's tavern, 79
Busch, Jacob, 119
Byer & Lantz, 106
Byer, Capt., 65
Byer, Elizabeth, 131
Byer, Frederick, 61, 106, 107, 137
Byer, Jacob, 65
Byer, John, 57, 64, 65, 92, 99, 100, 101, 103, 131, 132, 137
Calhoun, John C., 129
Cameron, Ludwig, 47
Campbell, J. F., 125
Carr, John, 73
Carroll, Charles of Bellvue, 54
Carroll, Charles, Major, 65
Carson, George, 152
Cass, Lewis, 61
Catens, Thomas, 25
Cavender, Charles, 144, 148
cemeteries, 141, 142
Chancellor, ___, 149
Chapline, ___, 10
Chapline, Joseph, 16
Charles, Rudolph, 95
Charlton, ___, 45, 51
Charlton, John, 27, 28, 73
Charlton, Poynton, 28, 27
Charlton, Thomas, 27
Chew's farm, 10
Church, John, 21
Claggett, Alexander, 40
Clay, Henry, 24
Cleaver, David, 89
Cleveland, Grover, 61
Cline, John P., 124, 132
Clopper, Henry, 50, 90, 151
Clopper, Henry G. 37, 53
Clopper, Simon, 29
Clopper, Upton, 36, 53, 111, 142
Clymer, Isaac, 103, 105
Cole, Susan, 131
Conrad, ___, 124
Conrad, F. W., 124, 125, 133
Conrad, Rev., 126
Cook, , Barbara, 131

Cook, H. S., 125
Cook, Mary, 126, 131
Cook, H. S., 125
Cook, Samuel, 86, 126, 142
Cook, Samuel (Mrs), 126
Cookston, Joseph, 138
Coon, ----, 67
Coons, Henry, 140
Copeigh, Augustus, 106
Cort, Cyrus, 23
Cost, Andrew, 139, 140
Coudy, James, 83
Coursey, John, 65
Crawford, Mr., 144
Creager, Jacob, 104
Creager, Samuel, 131
Creps, H. T., 111
Cresap, ___, 45, 51
Cresap, Col., 25
Cresap, Thomas, 21, 22, 29, 47, 62, 72
Cressler, ------, 24
Cressler, George A., 90
Crockett, Benjamin, 27
Crockett, John, 27
Cromer, See Kraumer.
Crooks, Dr., 107
Crumb, Mrs., 139
Darling, John, 26, 27, 65
Davis, Isaac E., 85
Davis, John, 150
Davis, Nathan, 65
Davis, Philip, 47
Dayhoff, Jacob, 140, 152
Dayhoff, John, 71, 141
Dayhoff, John S., 98
Deitrich, C. B., (Mrs) 49
Deitrich, David M., 68, 89, 94, 108
Delk, E. H., 125
Dent, J. P., 22
Dietzel, S. H., 134
Dillon, Michael, 90
Dilworth, Amos, 105
Dixon, Jeremiah, 46
Dizer, Peter, 73
Dorbart, John, 119

iii

Dornwart, Johannes, 119
Dorsett, John, 25
Dorsey, Edwin, 125
Dorsey, Frederick, 88, 151
Doub, Daniel 114
Douglass, Samuel, 39
Douglass, William, 38, 39, 47
Downin, S. S., 58, 85
Downing, Elizabeth, 114, 115
Downing, Esther, 113, 114, 115
Downing, James, 39, 73
Downing, Joseph, 115
Downing, Robert, 28, 29, 55, 69, 74, 99, 113, 114, 115
Downing, Samuel, 53, 55,
Doyle, William E, 59. 61, 62, 88, 100
Duckett, T. B., 60
Duckett, Thomas B., 107
Dulany, Daniel, 22, 35, 95
Dulany, Walter, 95
Duncan, Alexander, 119
Durboraw, Daniel, 27
Durboraw, Daniel W. 26, 99
Durboraw, Isaac H., 95
Eakle, John D., 85, 141, 153
Early, H. F., 124
Eastburn, Benjamin, 46
Ebrad, William, 120
Edwards, Emory, 83
Eichelberger, Samuel, 66
Elliott, John 148
Emerick, Ludwig, 119
Emmert, Joseph, 65, 139
Emmert, Leonard, 139
Eshleman, Christian, 138
Eshleman, Jacob, 90, 138
Eshleman, Jonas, 90
Eshleman, Joseph, 90, 138, 152
Eshleman, John, 33, 36, 39, 137
Eshleman, Peter, 89, 90, 138, 139, 152
Etnyer & Besore, 106
Etnyer & Martin, 106,
Etnyer, Samuel, 60, 68, 84, 94, 98, 106, 108, 131, 153

Eyster, W. F., 132
Farhney, Jeremiah, 94
Feirstien, Michael, 152
Fisk, Clinton B., 61
Fithian, Philip V., 16, 79
Fitzhugh, William H., 153
Flagg's crossing, 83
Fletcher & Good, 106
Fletcher, & Grimes, 106
Fletcher & Stonebraker, 104, 106
Fletcher & Lantz, 106
Fletcher, Elizabeth, 131
Fletcher, Charles A., 60, 68, 88, 104, 106
Flory, Christopher, 82
Flory, Wilfred L., 105, 107
Flory's [blacksmith] shop, 107
Fogler, Curtis, 27, 101
Fogler, Frederick, 35
Folger, Simon, 120
Forbush, George, 26, 27
Fore, Henry, 32, 38
Forney, ----, 67
Fouke, Henry, 82
Fowler & Ziegler's mill, 64, 84, 92, 99, 100
Fowler, Robert, 83, 88, 89, 100
Freed, Mayberry G., 133
French, Jacob, 35
French, Judge, 67
Frey, ____, 105, 106
Frey, Louisa, 131
Frick Co., 71
Frick, George, 71
Frick's foundry, 58
Fruhlig, ----, 119
Fry, John, 105
Fugate, Peter, 73
Fulk, Casper, 103
Funk, Jacob, 17, 63, 73, 77, 106, 137
Funk, Henry, 34, 39, 91, 137
Funk's mill, 83
Furnora, John, 97
Gabby, John, 44, 53, 64
Gabby, Joseph, 29, 34, 56, 60, 61,

Gabby, Joseph, 62, 87, 88, 99, 103, 104, 108, 137, 148
Gabby, William, 29, 35, 55, 56, 61, 62, 81, 103, 104, 137, 149, 153
Gagle, John, 67
Gagle, Henry, 107
Gagle, Solomon, 67
Gaither, Joseph, 78
Gallion, James, 152
Garfield, James A., 61
Garver, Anna (Snively), 152
Garver, Daniel, 67
Garver, Isaac, 38
Garver, Samuel, 34
Garver, Benjamin F., 67, 82, 84, 88, 89, 137, 153
Garver, Christian, 38, 79
Garver, Daniel, 67
Garver, Foltz & Co., 98
Garver, Jacob, 88, 147
Garver, John G., 132
Garver, Joseph, 84
Garvin, John, 104
Gelwix, James, 152
Geohagen, Ambrose, 44
Gilbert, David, 153
Gilbert, Jacob, 37, 94
Gilbert, Samuel, 25
Gilbert, Wendell, 25
Gilbert's mill, 94
Gladfelter, Edward, 67
Glessner, G. W., 134
Goll, Carl, 119
Goll, David, 120
Good, ___, 51
Good, Anna, 35
Good, Christian, 144, 147
Good, David M., 68, 89, 108
Good, Dr., 107
Good, Jacob, 25, 26, 31, 32, 35, 44, 45, 64, 72, 106, 136
Good, Jacob M., 101
Good, Peter, 35, 72
Grant, Ulysses S., 61
Grebill, Michael, 40

Grebill, Samuel, 73
Greeley, Horace, 61
Grider, Martin, 44
Grimes, Joshua, 68, 106, 130
Ground, Lewis J., 62
Ground, Josephus, 89, 104, 105, 106, 107, 108
Ground, Lewis J., 108
Grove, Jacob, 119
Growden, Lawrence, 46
Hafner, Albertus, 34
Hafner, Johannes, 119
Hagar, Jonathan, 16, 63, 73
Halbert, Archibald, 65
Haldimand, Frederick, 22, 23, 72
Hall, Letty, 55
Hall, Thomas, 54
Hall, Thomas B., 24, 61, 62
Hall, William, 30, 35
Hamilton, Alexander, 141
Hammaker, Isaac, 65
Hancock, Winfield S., 61
Harbaugh, John, 126, 133
Harbaugh, John (Mrs.), 105
Harman's gap, 147
Harne, Elisha, 150
Harpel, Jeremiah, 125
Harper, Charles W., 105
Harper, Dr., 107
Harper's Ferry, 16
Harris's Ferry, 15
Harrison, Benjamin, 61
Harrison, William Henry, 61
Harrison, President, 60
Harry, George I., 39, 56, 152, 153
Harry, John, 81, 82
Harshman, Upton W., 33
Hart, Thomas, 23, 24, 25, 61
Hartle, ___, 26
Hartle, Claggett A., 111
Hartle, Clinton, 136
Hartle, Daniel T., 111
Hartle, Frederick, 31, 44
Hartle, George, 30, 44, 69
Hartle, Harvey J., 26, 53, 91, 111
Hartle, Henry, 31, 84

v

Hartle, Jacob, 135
Hartle, John, 26
Hartle, Levi, 26, 101
Hartle, Martin, 31
Hartle, Samuel, 31
Hartle, Sebastian, 40,
Hartle, Solomon, 135
Hartle, Susanna, 131
Hartman, Andrew, 106, 107
Hartman, Benjamin, 59, 62
Hartman, Samuel, 68, 93
Hartness, Robert, 30, 35
Hartwick, J. G., 115
Hauks, Thomas, 143, 144
Haushihl, Bernard Michael, 115
Haushihl, Pastor, 113
Hawbecker, John, 140
Hayes, Rutherford B., 61
Hays, Abner, 60, 131
Hays, James A., 62, 67, 68, 108, 111
Hays, Levan, 91
Hays, Mary, 131
Heck, John, 124, 125, 132
Heinrich, Johnan, 121
Hellman, Joshua, 67
Hendricks, Alfred, 106
Herbert, Hilary, 150
Hicks, D. J. D., 107, 108, 133
Hicks, Daniel J. D., 105
High, David V., 67
Hilbarger, Jacob, 139
Hockman, H. B., 37
Hockman, Henry B., 53
Hoffman, ----, 136
Hoffman, Jacob, 137
Hoffman, William H., 38, 49, 142,
Hoffmeyer, Rev., 124
Hogmire, Jonas, 45
Hogmire, Conrad, 63, 73, 77
Hollinger, C. C., 35, 36
Hoover, ___, 136
Hoover, Andrew, 32, 74
Hoover, Catharine, 131
Hoover, Christopher, 140
Hoover, Daniel, 33, 34

Hoover, David, 64, 108, 137
Hoover, Jacob, 132
Hoover, John, 134, 137, 140
Hoover, Peter, 137
Horine, M. C., 132
Horst, John, 34
Horst, ___, 83
Horst, Christian, 138
Horst, John, 137
Horst, Michael, 139
Hoser, Isaac, 73
Hoshour, Samuel K., 132
Hotel Cross Keys, 014
Houser, Jacob, 103
Houser, Samuel, 104
Hovis, Jacob, 67
Howard, Frederick, 79
Huber, Jacob, 119
Hughes, ___, 10
Hughes, Col., 40
Hughes, Daniel, 27, 40, 43, 95. 96, 97,
Hughes, Holker, 98
Hughes, Robert, 40, 81, 82, 85,
Hughes, Thomas, 67
Hughes, Samuel, 23, 39, 72, 96
Humphreys, Jonathan, 106, 141
Huyett, Jacob, 82
Hykes, Isaac, 39, 47
Hykes, J. H., 39
Hykes, Jacob, 140
Hykes, Mary A., 31, 32
Hykes, Samuel, 53
Hykes, W. Harvey, 31, 40
Hyple, Christian, 37, 94
Ingram, Edward, 85
Ingram, John, 63
Irwin, Samuel, 47
Jacob, Anna Maria, 121
Jacob, Heinrich, 121
Jacob, Johan Heinrich, 119, 121
Jacobs, Daniel, 39, 65, 140
Jacobs, David, 45
Jacobs, George, 122
Jacobs, Henry, 97, 126, 148
Jacobs, Henry E., 117

cobs, Henry M., 31, 32
cobs, John, 125, 126
cobs, Martin, 119, 121, 122
cobs, Melinda B., 125
cques, ------, 10, 11
rb, Henry, 119
)hns, Thomas, 39S
)hnson, Daniel T., 111
)hnson, Dr., 106
)hnson, Jacob, 40
)hnson, James. 105, 107
)hnson, John, 36, 141
)hnson, William, 105
)nes, Chatham, 56
ahl, Otho, 126
eedy, C. L., 125
eller, E., 124
eeler, George, 39
eller, John, 73
elly, William, 73
ent, Joseph, 129
ercheval, _____, 52
essinger, George, 84, 103, 104
essinger, George, Jr., 153
essinger, Jacob, 55
essinger, Mrs., 105
ieffer, J. Spangler, 135
ieffer, John D., 131
imler, Joseph, 85
inkle, Adam, 93
issel & Metz, 106
issel, Jacob, 68, 131
issel, John, 131
line, Rev., 126
line, Samuel, 67
line, William, 67
oons, Henry, 139
oppisch. See also Copeigh
oppisch, Frederick, 68
oppisch, Charles E. H., 67, 68
oppisch. See Copeigh.
raumer, Samuel, 44, 94
reps, William, 62, 106
reps, William H., 31
riner, John, 40
roh, Henry, 130, 134, 135

Kurtz, Benjamin, 130, 132
Kurtz, Jr., 116
Kurtz, Senior, 116
Lahm, George W., 106
Lahm, John, 37, 62, 104, 106, 132
Lahm, Samuel, 131
Lambert, ____51,
Lambert, Eva, 141
Lambert, George, 28, 37, 64, 73,
Lambert, George H., 62, 137
Lambert, J. D., 135, 136
Lambert, Jacob, 144, 147
Lambert, John, 37, 62
Lantz, Adam, 103, 104
Lantz, Capt., 65
Lantz, Christian, 26, 44, 55, 63, 72,
    103, 119, 121, 131
Lantz, Christian, Jr., 92
Lantz, Elizabeth, 131
Lantz, G. W., 112
Lantz, George, 44, 53, 92, 103, 119
Oliver F., 27
Lantz, Samuel, 100, 106, 131, 137
Lantz, William M., 62
Lantz's mill, 85
Lauman, Eva, 121
Lauman, Martin, 121
Lauman, Regina Elizabeth, 121
Lawrence, Upton, 87
Leather, Ida, 141
Leather, Margaret (Mrs), 36
Leatherman, Michael, 30
Lecron, Lewis, 32, 40
Lee, General, 66
Lee, William, 78
Lehman, ____, 90
Lehman, Abraham, 24
Lehman, Christian, 91
Lehman, Henry F., 84, 93
Lehman, Jacob B., 25, 93
Lehman, John F., 85
Leiter, ____, 51
Leiter, Abraham, 34
Leiter, Andreas, 121
Leiter, Andrew, 101, 103, 104, 107.
    141

Leiter, Ann, 105
Leiter, Anna, 35
Leiter, Anna Maria, 131
Leiter, Barbara, 105, 121, 131
Leiter, Barbara A., 131
Leiter, Catharine, 131
Leiter, Christian, 31, 32, 79, 94
Leiter, Elizabeth, 131
Leiter, George, Sr., 120
Leiter, Henry, 152
Leiter, Isaac G., 107
Leiter, Isabella, 131
Leiter, J. F., 141
Leiter, Jacob, 25, 31, 32, 35, 44, 69, 72, 92, 94, 99, 101, 102, 121, 141
Leiter, Jacob, Sr., 119
Leiter, J. Freeland, 61, 108
Leiter, Joseph, 59, 61, 69, 89, 105, 107, 108, 124
Leiter, Julianna, 121
Leiter, Martha H., 33, 34
Leiter, L. Z., 141
Leiter, Peter, 32, 44, 94, 102
Leiter, Samuel, 104, 107, 131
Leiter, Susan, 131
Leiter, Susanna Catharina, 121
Lepley, Christian, 131, 152
Lesher, Jacob, 137
Lesher, John, 137
Levering, Joshua, 61
Light, Barnhart B., 101, 104
Light, John, 104
Light, Samuel, 105, 106
Lightcap, Jacob, 152
Lloyd, James, 87
Logan, Hugh, 60, 62
Logan, William, 62
Long, Joseph, 26, 44, 72
Lowman, Catharine, 131
Lowman, Daniel, 103, 104, 105, 106, 112
Lowman, George U., 67
Lowman, Jacob F., 67
Lowman, John, 105
Lowman, Keller, 67

Lowman, Mary A., 131
Lyday, Adam. 119
Lyday, Samuel, 59, 60, 61, 62, 83, 88, 91, 98, 106
Magill, William D., 24
Malott, Daniel, 82
Mangle, Jacob, 131
Marshall, J., 24
Martin, Abraham H., 136, 137
Martin, Catharine, 131
Martin, D. G., 60
Martin, Daniel, 33
Martin, Henry, 33
Martin, Immanuel, 36, 80, 99
Martin, Jacob, 125
Martin, John, 131, 138
Martin, John, Jr., 85
Martin, Joseph, 28, 141
Martin, Kate E., 36, 80, 99, 133
Martin, Nicholas, 73
Martin, Samuel, 30, 32, 36, 37, 72, 75, 91, 98
Martin, Stephen, 95, 99, 133, 147
Martz, Jacob, 105
Maugans, Martin, 66
May, Jacob, 119
Mayhew, James P., 61, 62, 69, 131, 132
Mayhew, Mary, 131
McAtee, William B., 108
McCausland, ----, 13
McClelland, John, 40
McConkey, John, 23, 24, 72
McDowell, Nathan, 88, 112
McDowell, Samuel, 105
McGeecham, ____, 149
McHenry, Samuel, 132
McKee, John, 148
McKinley, WIlliam, 61
McPherson, J., 66
McVey, John, 65
Medtart, Jacob, 130, 132
Meek, Thomas, 47
Mentzer, Catharine, 37, 131
Mentzer, Daniel, 62, 89, 91, 153
Mentzer, E. Keller, 38, 53

Mentzer, Jacob B., 105
Mentzer, John, 38, 53, 85, 88, 119, 152, 153
Mentzer, John, Jr., 55
Mentzer, Joseph S., 126
Mentzer, Lewis L., 101
Mentzer, Walter S., 126
Mero, Frederick, 120
Metz, Catharine, 131
Metz, Jacob A., 66
Metz, Joseph A., 108
Middlekauff, Hiram D., 29, 35, 53, 99
Middlekauff, J. P., 136
Middlekauff, John, 135
Middlekauff, Joseph, 85
Middlekauff, Peter, 62, 89, 90, 134, 135
Middlekauff, Samuel, 111
Miller, ___, 67
Miller, Catharine, 136
Miller, Elizabeth, 131
Miller, Frank, 105
Miller, Henry, 105, 119
Miller, J. O., 135
Miller, Jacob, 31, 55, 66, 89, 136, 137, 150, 152
Miller, John, 135, 140, 152
Miller, John C., 31, 139
Miller, John H., 47, 50, 135
Miller, Jos., 65
Miller, Joseph, 53, 93, 150
Miller, Josephine, 133
Miller, Mary E., 133
Miller, Michael, 25, 30, 72, 136
Miller, S. S., 135
Miller, Samuel, 65
Miller, V., 124
Miller, Victor, 132, 133
Miller, Virgil H., 107. 111
Minor, Frank, 105
Minor, Henry, 105
Minor, Samuel 105, 107
Minor, William, 65
Mitchell, Joseph, 78
Mong, Peter, 82

Moore, George, 73
Mort, Elizabeth, 131
Motter, I. N., 135
Mouer's mill, 81
Mowen, Daniel, 33
Mowry, Abram, 67
Mowry, John, 67
Mowry, Polk, 67
Moxley, Virgil, 24
Moyer, Abraham, 37, 94, 99
Moyer, John, 144, 147
Mueller, George Adam, 143
Muhlenburg, Frederick [Augustus], 116
Muhlenburg, Henry Melchoir, 115
Myers, Henry, 39, 104, 140
Myers, Martin, 18
Myers, Samuel, 104
Myers, Solomon, 67
Neal's meadow, 22
Needy, Isaac, 36, 37
Negro, Betty, 55
Negro, Bob, 55
Negro, Dick, 55
Negro, Jem, 55
Negro, Jemima, 56
Negro, Kate, 55
Negro, Rachel, 55
Negro, Will, 55
Neill, Alexander, 89
Newcomer, Andrew, 66, 137
Newcomer, Christian, 137, 138
Newcomer, Emma S., 133
Newcomer, Jacob, 66, 137
Newcomer, John, 66, 137, 150
Newcomer, John B., 27
Newcomer, Mary M., 38, 152
Newcomer, Peter, 137, 147
Newcomer, Samuel, 72
Newman, John, 150
Nicodemus, Frederick, 119
Nicodemus, John, 13
Nigh, John, 68
Nigh, John W., 67, 111
Nigh, Samuel, 153
Nigh, Samuel T., 67

Niuffer, Michael, 107
Noffard, Gabby, 67
Nofford, John, 131
Norrison, John, 55
Oaks, Henry, 126
Oberholtzer, Jacob, 89, 90, 138
Ogle, Govenor, 45
Ogle, Samuel, 21
Oller, Daniel, 36, 37, 99
O'Neal, Lawrence, 43, 95
Oswald, David, 84
Oswald, John, 84, 147
Oswald, P., 85
Palmer, John R, 61
Pawling, Samuel, 73
Perry, ___ 51
Perry, Joseph, 27, 34, 63, 64
Peters, Richard, 46
Petre, Amy, 139
Petre, George, 151
Petre, George W., 139, 140
Petre, Margaret, 139
Pfeiffer, Christian, 119
Phillips, Thomas, 93
Phillips, Samuel, 152
Pierce, Franklin, 61
Piper, E. E., 85
Poe, Charles E., 107
Poe, George, 29, 30, 31, 33, 36, 60, 62, 72, 83, , 84, 102, 104, 107, 112, 137, 139
Poe, Mark Z., 143
Poe's smith shop, 107
Pole, George W., 61, 89, 102, 108
Polk, James K., 61
Prather, Thomas, 47, 73, 78
Price, Aaron, 73
Price, Samuel, 107
Probst, J. F., 132
Protzman, Joseph G., 131
Protzman, Sarah, 131
Purviance, Samuel, 96
Ragan, Richard. 24
Reck, John, 132
Reed, Hannah, 55
Reiff, Andrew, 136

Reiff, John, 25, 26, 32, 44
Reiff, Joseph, Sr., 137
Reinall, Philip, 32
Rench, Capt., 65
Rench, Jacob, 81
Rench, John, 24, 25, 93, 72
Rench, Peter, 25, 73, 93
Rench, Thomas H., 150
Rench's mill, 79. 85, 93
Repp, Catharine, 131
Repp, Elizabeth, 105
Repp, John, 131
Repp, Michael, 131
Repp, Peter. 131
Reynolds, John, 103
Reynolds, Maria E. (Mrs), 56
Richardson, X. J., 124, 132
Ridenour, ___, 115
Ridenour, Martin, 114
Rider, Jacob, 120
Riemensnyder, John J., 132
Right, Richard, 27
Riley, ___, 67
Ringgold, Samuel, 64
Ringgold's Manor, 10
Ripple, Philip, 119, 120
Ritter, ___, 51
Ritter, David, 119
Ritter, Jacob, 32, 64, 119, 131
Ritter, John, 73
Ritter, Mary, 131
Rochester, Nathaniel, 23
Rohrer. Catharine, 105
Rohrer, John, 73, 77, 114
Rohrer, William H., 84
Rohrer's mill, 114
Roland, David, 138
Rolls, William N., 59
Rook, David, 131
Rook, John, 131
Ross, John, 126
Ross, Joseph, 131
Roth, Abraham, 138
Rowe, John, 140
Rowland, Abram, 139
Rowland, Daniel, 139

x

Rowland, Daniel G., 89, 90
Rowland, Jonas, 139
Rowland, John, 139, 140
Russell, Christian, 94, 103
Russell, John, 94
Russell, Christian, 103, 133
Ruthrauff, Frederick, 130
Ruthrauff, Henry, 131
Ruthrauff, Jacob, 131
Ruthrauff, John, 118, 119, 120, 121, 125, 130, 132
Ruthrauff, Susan, 131
Sahm, ----, 124
Sahm, Peter, 125
Santee, J. W., 134
Santee, Charles A, 134, 135
Santee, J. W., 135
Scheetz, Daniel, 137
Scheller, ___, 90
Scheller, Daniel N., 28, 53, 75, 90 139, 140, 142
Schilling, Frederick, 131
Schilling, Julia A, 131
Schlatter, ___, 10
Schlatter, Susanna, 96
Schlencker, Daniel, 150
Schlencker, Henry, 150
Schmutz, Abraham, 65, 82, 93
Schmutz, Jacob, 150
Schmutz's mill, 64, 151
Schnebley, Henry, 23, 33, 34, 39, 63, 69, 72,
Schnebley, Jacob, 39, 56, 81
Schnebley, John, 35
Schriver, ---, 83
Schriver, Henry, 33, 34, 83, 84, 111, 137, 153
Schriver, John, 34
Schwerdtfeger, Pastor, 113
Schwerdtfeger, William Samuel, 115
Scott, John, 37
Scott, Winfield, 61
Seibert, Peter, 153
Senger, Leonard, 40
Seymour, Horatio. 61
Shafer, Nicholas, 37

Shamhart, Henry, 104
Shanaberger, Peter, 94
Shanafield, ___, 117
Shanafield, William, 114, 115
Shank, ANdrew, Jr., 147
Shank, Andrew M., 84, 99 , 137
Shank, Christian, 136, 137, 138
Shank, Daniel, 137
Shank, Daniel V., 40
Shank, Frederick, 138
Shank, Henry, 136, 139, 140
Shank, Isaac, 39, 53, 99,
Shank, Jacob, 137, 147
Shank, Jonas, 137
Shank, Joseph, 33
Shank, Noah E., 31, 150
Sharpe, Gov., 11
Sharpe, Horatio, 16
Shatzer, John, 107
Sheetz, Daniel, 105
Sheetz, John, 131
Sheetz, Mary A., 131
Shelby, Capt [Evan], 49
Shelby, Isaac, 48
Shiess, Francis C., 62, 147
Shiess, George, 34, 56, 99, 104, 137
Shiess, Peter, 29, 32, 33, 35, 40 44, 64, 69, 72, 91
Shiess, William, 105
Shiess, William L., 107
Shiffler, Augustus, 49
Shockey, Benjamin, 97, 99
Shockey, Stophel, 47
Shoemaker, David B., 49
Shook, John, 131
Shoup, Barton, 139
Shriver, Henry, 71, 83, 84
Shutt, John, 107
Siekman, ___, 105, 106
Sights, Wendell, 38, 64, 69
Simpson, John, 34
Sittro, Davis, 120
Slaughenhaupt, James D., 62
Slick, Benjamin F., 68
Slick, James, 105

xi

Slick, Jeremiah, 112
Slick, Robert, 67
Slush, Andrew, 38
Smith, Christopher, 17
Smith, Edward, 62, 111, 141
Smith, Henry, 36, 141
Smith, John, 45
Smith, John William, 73
Smith, Joseph, 55
Smith, Thomas, 147
Snell, Henry, 36, 79
Snell, Philip, 36
Snider, Catharine, 131
Snider, Henry, 131
Snider, Henry H., 132
Snider, Henry, 106
Snively, Andrew, 137
Snively, Henry H., 91
Snively, John, 137
Sniveley's sawmill, 90
Solmes, Catharine, 37
Solmes, Henry, 37, 44
Solmes, Margaret, 37
South, Daniel, 83
Spessard, B. F., 135
Spessard, John, 142
Spessard, Iva, 136
Spessard, Peter, 58
Spitzer, Elizabeth, 131
Sprigg, ___, 51, 56,
Sprigg, Daniel, 39
Sprigg, Gen., 53. 93
Sprigg, Joseph, 23, 24, 39, 72,
Sprigg, Joseph, Jr., 78
Sprigg, Maria E., 56
Sprigg, T., Gen., 65
Sprigg, Thomas, 24, 56, 61, 62, 54, 64, 99
Sprigg, William O., 61, 81
St. John, John P., 61
Staley, Alice M., 111
Staley, Stephen G., 106
Startzman, ___, 124
Stauffer, Jacob, 111
Stephey, David, 67
Stephey, John P., 59, 60

Stephey, William, 67
Stevens, Thaddeus, 75
Stevenson, William H., 27, 142, 152
Stockslager, ___, 25
Stockslager, Alveh L., 26, 31, 142
Stoff, Maria, 131
Stolz, Herman, 119
Stonehouse, Henry, 141
Stoner, ___, 26
Stoner, Abraham, 38
Stoner, David, 38
Stoner, Elizabeth, (Mrs) 27
Stoner, Jacob B., 27, 95
Stoner, John, 27, 38, 40
Stoner, Martin, 140
Stoner's mill, 73, 90
Story, Joseph, 24
Stotler, Catharine, 38
Stotler, Peter, 37, 38, 44, 140
Stottlemeyer, Elias R., 94
Stouffer, Abraham, 37, 94, 137, 153
Stouffer, Abraham, Jr., 137
Stouffer, Christian, 137
Stouffer, Daniel F., 139, 140
Stouffer, Jacob. 124
Stouffer, Jacob M., 68, 124, 197
Stouffer, John, 66
Strite, Abraham, 65, 74, 83, 84, 88, 89, 153, 154
Strite, Abraham, (Mrs.), 33
Strite, Abram, 108
Strite, Andre, 143
Strite, Andrew, 143
Strite, Catharine, 99
Strite, Christian, 88, 89, 95, 108, 138, 152
Strite, David, 31, 89, 98, 108, 138
Strite, Fanny, 40
Strite, Franklin M., 33, 34, 49, 99
Strite, Henry L., 31
Strite, John, 36, 40, 65, 136, 137, 138, 152
Strite, John C., 95, 107
Strite, John F., 31, 40, 86
Strite, John S., 33, 35, 138
Strite, Johannes, 137

Strite, Joseph, 29, 31, 35, 53, 65, 79, 137, 138, 153
Strite, Joseph (Mrs) 81
Strite, Lt., 67
Strite, Samuel, 62, 65, 89, 95, 103, 108, 137, 152
Strite's mill, 81, 94, 107
Strock, William B., 84
Stull, Col., 64
Stull's mill, 14, 15, 73, 90
Summer, David, 111
Summer, John, 136
Summer, Thomas, 136
Summers, Michael, 119
Summers, Matthias, 120
Swaddinger's Ferry, 47
Swearingen, Joseph, 73
Swenk, Casper, 37
Tanner, Jacob, 130
Taylor, Ignatius, 39, 54, 61, 62,
Taylor, Zachary, 61
Tharpe, Jacob, 79
Tice, Henry, 73
Tidball, Robert M., 88
Tilden, Samuel J., 61
Tritle, Catharine, 131
Tritle, Daniel, 67
Tritle, Jacob, 98
Tritle, Lewis, 60, 130, 131
Trovinger, Christopher, 85
Trovinger, Frank, 68
Trovinger, Joseph, 59, 60, 65, 114, 150
Trovinger, Samuel, 139
Trovinger, William R., 68
Trovinger's mill, 29, 63
Turner, Robert, 73
Uhler, John, 126
Unclesby, Hilary, 105, 107,
VanBuren, Martin, 61
VanSwearingen,____, Jr., 78
Volgemore, Joseph, 73
Waggoner, Maggie P., 111
Wagner, Felix, 119
Wagner, Frederick, 120
Walgamot' mill, 14, 15

Walker, Michael, 47
Wall, Henry, 73
Walling, James, 73
Walter, C. L., 126
Walter, C. L. (Mrs), 126
Walter, Henry, 44
Walter, John, 126
Walter, Meta, 126
Wampler, John, 67
Warfield, Philip (Mrs), 139
Washabaugh, Dilman, 73
Watkins Ferry, 47
Weaver, J., 87
Weaver, James, 59
Weaver, Lewis, 103
Webb, William, 60, 62
Wellar, Capt., 65
Welty, ____, 136
Welty, B. F., 73, 90
Welty, John, 82, 84, 87, 137, 138, 153
Wesenman, John, 119
White, Dr., 107
White, Edward M., 31
Wildbahn, [Charles Frederick], 115, 116
William's Ferry,
Williams, Otho Holland, 17, 87
Wilms, F. C. B., 56
Wilson, David T., 59
Wilson, D. T., 65
Wilson, David, T., 59
Wingardt, Guenther, 118, 125
Winrode, ____, 149
Winter, Daniel, 27, 95, 153
Winters, ____, 35
Wishard, J. H., 86, 107
Wishard, Jacob, 99
Wishard, John, 28
Wishard, Joseph, 36, 37
Wolf, John (Mrs), 105
Wolf, Joseph, 139
Wolfersberger, John, 58, 65
Wolff, Garrett, 137
Wolfinger, Charles B., 27, 106
Wolfinger, Daniel, 111

Wolfinger, Daniel S., 33, 53, 68
Wolfinger, David, 131
Wolfinger, Elizabeth, 131
Wolfinger, George H., 134
Wolfinger, Harry, 136
Wolfinger, Jacob, 131
Wolfinger, Jacob D., 111, 131
Wolfinger, John O., 153
Wolfinger, Levi B., 27
Wolfinger, Michael, 32, 53, 81, 85, 99, 120, 120, 131
Wolfinger, Sarah, 131
Wolgamot. See Volgemore, 73
Wolgamot's mill, 90
Yesler, Catharine, 38
Yesler, Henry, 38, 131, 140, 141
Yesler, Peter, 141
Yost, D. G., 93
Young, John George, 113, 115, 116, 118
Young, Ludwig, 78
Young, William S. (Mrs), 22, 24
Zeller, Jacob, 63
Ziegler, George L., 61
Ziegler, ___ 25
Ziegler, Abigail, 136
Ziegler, Alice, 68, 136
Ziegler, Catharine, 131
Ziegler, Charles C., 107, 111
Ziegler, David, 58, 64, 79, 93, 142
Ziegler, Frederick, 39, 57, 58, 60, 67, 87, 88, 93, 99, 103, 130, 131, 132, 149
Ziegler, Frederick K., 61, 62, 100
Ziegler, George, 61, 67, 94, 103, 133, 141, 144
Ziegler, George F., 53, 99, 141
Ziegler, George L., 61, 88, 89, 108
Ziegler, George W., 112, 131, 142, 142
Ziegler, Jacob A., 135
Zieglerr, James H., 111
Ziegler, James R., 67
Ziegler, John, 107
Ziegler, John H., 68,

Ziegler, Laura K., 105
Ziegler, Lewis, 57, 60, 61, 65, 87 88, 99, 105, 108, 130, 131 137, 139, 153
Ziegler, Louisa, 105
Ziegler, Madaline, 131
Ziegler, Samuel, 68
Ziegler, Samuel F., 62, 68, 106, 10
Ziegler, Sophia, 142
Ziegler's mill, 74, 82

www.ingramcontent.com/pod-product-compliance
Lightning Source LLC
Chambersburg PA
CBHW062223080426
42734CB00010B/2009